Instructor's Manual to Accompany
MANAGERIAL ACCOUNTING

Second Edition

Cecily A. Raiborn
Loyola University—New Orleans

Jesse T. Barfield
Loyola University—New Orleans

Michael R. Kinney
Texas A&M University

Prepared by
Gregory K. Lowry

West Publishing Company
Minneapolis/St. Paul   New York   Los Angeles   San Francisco

WEST'S COMMITMENT TO THE ENVIRONMENT

In 1906, West Publishing Company began recycling materials left over from the production of books. This began a tradition of efficient and responsible use of resources. Today, up to 95% of our legal books and 70% of our college texts and school texts are printed on recycled, acid-free stock. West also recycles nearly 22 million pounds of scrap paper annually—the equivalent of 181,717 trees. Since the 1960s, West has devised ways to capture and recycle waste inks, solvents, oils, and vapors created in the printing process. We also recycle plastics of all kinds, wood, glass, corrugated cardboard, and batteries, and have eliminated the use of Styrofoam book packaging. We at West are proud of the longevity and the scope of our commitment to the environment.

Production, Prepress, Printing and Binding by West Publishing Company.

 TEXT IS PRINTED ON 10% POST CONSUMER RECYCLED PAPER   PRINTED WITH SOY INK

CONTENTS

PREFACE

This instructor's manual is designed to be a teaching supplement to
MANAGERIAL ACCOUNTING, SECOND EDITION by Cecily A. Raiborn,
Jesse T. Barfield, and Michael R. Kinney. The manual is prepared as an aid for
instructors in teaching managerial accounting. Each chapter in the text has a
corresponding chapter in the manual.

SAMPLE SYLLABI are furnished for the use of instructors. Sample syllabi are
presented in sixteen chapter, fourteen chapter, and twelve chapter formats.

LEARNING OBJECTIVES at the beginning of each chapter present a list of the
major objectives of the chapter. After reading and studying each chapter, a
student should be able to discuss each of the topics listed.

A TERMINOLOGY SECTION provides definitions of the key terms in each
chapter for use by the instructor as a lecture aid or as a handout for students.

A LECTURE OUTLINE covers each chapter in enough detail to make the outline
an effective lecture aid for the instructor.

MULTIPLE CHOICE QUESTIONS FROM CMA EXAMINATIONS are
provided at the end of each chapter – except for chapters 1 and 2. The questions
may be used by the instructor as additional or supplementary examination
questions, or as extra credit projects for students. Permission has been obtained
from the Institute of Management Accountants to use questions and/or
unofficial answers from past CMA examinations.

TEACHING TRANSPARENCY MASTERS are provided for the convenience of
the instructor in order to illustrate various key points or accounting flows
throughout the text.

SAMPLE SYLLABI

SIXTEEN CHAPTER SYLLABUS I

CHAPTER	TOPIC TO BE COVERED	SUGGESTED ASSIGNMENT
1	Management Accounting in a Global Business Environment	Question 3, 8, 13, 15 Exercise 23, 25, 27, 28 Case 38
2	Management Accounting in Quality-Oriented Environment	Question 1, 5, 7, 13, 17, 20 Exercise 24, 28 Case 33
3	Cost Terminology and Cost Flows	Question 2, 4, 5, 6, 8, 11, 14 Exercise 21, 22, 25, 28, 30, 36, 37 Problem 42, 44, 46, 50 Case 54
4	Including Overhead in Product and Service Costs	Question 1, 4, 8, 10, 11, 17, 22 Exercise 24, 25, 28, 31, 33, 37, 39 Problem 44, 46, 47, 49, 52, 55, 57 Case 58

EXAM 1 – Chapters 1-4

CHAPTER	TOPIC TO BE COVERED	SUGGESTED ASSIGNMENT
5	Activity-Based Management	Question 2, 3, 6, 9, 11, 15, 20 Exercise 21, 22, 25, 26, 30 Problem 39, 43, 44 Case 45
6	Introduction to a Standard Cost System	Question 1, 5, 6, 9, 12, 17, 20, 21 Exercise 22, 23, 26, 28, 31, 32, 33 Problem 40, 42, 43, 47 Case 52
7	Process Costing	Question 1, 5, 10, 14, 20, 23 Exercise 25, 26, 31, 32, 34 Problem 40, 43, 44, 45, 46 Case 48
8	Variable Costing and Cost-Volume-Profit Analysis	Question 1, 4, 10, 15, 24 Exercise 26, 30, 34, 36, 41, 43, 48 Problem 60, 62, 64, 66, 71 Case 73

EXAM 2 – Chapters 5-8

CHAPTER	TOPIC TO BE COVERED	SUGGESTED ASSIGNMENT
9	Relevant Costing	Question 1, 4, 8, 12, 17, 23, 24 Exercise 25, 28, 30, 32, 33, 36, 37 Problem 43, 46, 47, 48, 49, 50, 53 Case 55
10	Managerial Aspects of Budgeting	Question 1, 6, 11, 16, 22, 23 Exercise 24, 25, 26, 27, 30, 31 Problem 40, 41 Case 42
11	The Master Budget	Question 2, 5, 6, 7, 10, 16, 19, 20 Exercise 22, 23, 25, 28, 29, 30, 31 Problem 36, 37, 39, 40, 42, 44 Case 45
12	Controlling Noninventory Costs	Question 3, 6, 8, 10, 12, 14, 18 Exercise 19, 21, 23, 26, 29, 32 Problem 38, 40, 42, 43, 44, 47, 48 Case 49

EXAM 3 – Chapters 9-12

CHAPTER	TOPIC TO BE COVERED	SUGGESTED ASSIGNMENT
13	Controlling Inventory and Production Costs	Question 1, 5, 9, 12, 16, 20, 22 Exercise 23, 24, 25, 30, 31, 32, 33 Problem 42, 43, 46, 48, 49, 51 Case 52
14	Capital Asset Selection and Capital Budgeting	Question 2, 6, 9, 13, 17, 19, 25 Exercise 28, 30, 32, 35, 38, 39, 42 Problem 50, 52, 54, 58, 59, 62, 65 Case 66
15	Responsibility Accounting and Transfer Pricing in Decentralized Operations	Question 1, 5, 6, 8, 13, 15, 18, 19 Exercise 21, 23, 24, 27, 28, 31, 34 Problem 41, 42, 43, 44, 46, 47, 50 Case 51
16	Measuring and Rewarding Performance	Question 1, 5, 6, 10, 14, 15, 19 Exercise 24, 28, 30, 32, 35, 36, 37 Problem 47, 48, 49, 50, 51, 53 Case 54

EXAM 4 – Chapters 13-16

Review for Final Exam

COMPREHENSIVE FINAL EXAM

SIXTEEN CHAPTER SYLLABUS II

CHAPTER	TOPIC TO BE COVERED	SUGGESTED ASSIGNMENT
1	Management Accounting in a Global Business Environment	Question 3, 8, 13, 15 Exercise 23, 25, 27, 28 Case 38
2	Management Accounting in Quality-Oriented Environment	Question 1, 5, 7, 13, 17, 20 Exercise 24, 28 Case 33
3	Cost Terminology and Cost Flows	Question 2, 4, 5, 6, 8, 11, 14 Exercise 21, 22, 25, 28, 30, 36, 37 Problem 42, 44, 46, 50 Case 54
4	Including Overhead in Product and Service Costs	Question 1, 4, 8, 10, 11, 17, 22 Exercise 24, 25, 28, 31, 33, 37, 39 Problem 44, 46, 47, 49, 52, 55, 57 Case 58

EXAM 1 – Chapters 1-4

CHAPTER	TOPIC TO BE COVERED	SUGGESTED ASSIGNMENT
9	Relevant Costing	Question 1, 4, 8, 12, 17, 23, 24 Exercise 25, 28, 30, 32, 33, 36, 37 Problem 43, 46, 47, 48, 49, 50, 53 Case 55
10	Managerial Aspects of Budgeting	Question 1, 6, 11, 16, 22, 23 Exercise 24, 25, 26, 27, 30, 31 Problem 40, 41 Case 42
11	The Master Budget	Question 2, 5, 6, 7, 10, 16, 19, 20 Exercise 22, 23, 25, 28, 29, 30, 31 Problem 36, 37, 39, 40, 42, 44 Case 45
12	Controlling Noninventory Costs	Question 3, 6, 8, 10, 12, 14, 18 Exercise 19, 21, 23, 26, 29, 32 Problem 38, 40, 42, 43, 44, 47, 48 Case 49

EXAM 2 – Chapters 9-12

CHAPTER	TOPIC TO BE COVERED	SUGGESTED ASSIGNMENT
6	Introduction to a Standard Cost System	Question 1, 5, 6, 9, 12, 17, 20, 21 Exercise 22, 23, 26, 28, 31, 32, 33 Problem 40, 42, 43, 47 Case 52
7	Process Costing	Question 1, 5, 10, 14, 20, 23 Exercise 25, 26, 31, 32, 34 Problem 40, 43, 44, 45, 46 Case 48
8	Variable Costing and Cost-Volume-Profit Analysis	Question 1, 4, 10, 15, 24 Exercise 26, 30, 34, 36, 41, 43, 48 Problem 60, 62, 64, 66, 71 Case 73
15	Responsibility Accounting and Transfer Pricing in Decentralized Operations	Question 1, 5, 6, 8, 13, 15, 18, 19 Exercise 21, 23, 24, 27, 28, 31, 34 Problem 41, 42, 43, 44, 46, 47, 50 Case 51

EXAM 3 – Chapters 6-8, 15

13	Controlling Inventory and Production Costs	Question 1, 5, 9, 12, 16, 20, 22 Exercise 23, 24, 25, 30, 31, 32, 33 Problem 42, 43, 46, 48, 49, 51 Case 52
14	Capital Asset Selection and Capital Budgeting	Question 2, 6, 9, 13, 17, 19, 25 Exercise 28, 30, 32, 35, 38, 39, 42 Problem 50, 52, 54, 58, 59, 62, 65 Case 66
5	Activity-Based Management	Question 2, 3, 6, 9, 11, 15, 20 Exercise 21, 22, 25, 26, 30 Problem 39, 43, 44 Case 45
16	Measuring and Rewarding Performance	Question 1, 5, 6, 10, 14, 15, 19 Exercise 24, 28, 30, 32, 35, 36, 37 Problem 47, 48, 49, 50, 51, 53 Case 54

EXAM 4 – Chapters 13-14, 5, 16

Review for Final Exam

COMPREHENSIVE FINAL EXAM

FOURTEEN CHAPTER SYLLABUS

CHAPTER	TOPIC TO BE COVERED	SUGGESTED ASSIGNMENT
1	Management Accounting in a Global Business Environment	Question 3, 8, 13, 15 Exercise 23, 25, 27, 28 Case 38
2	Management Accounting in Quality-Oriented Environment	Question 1, 5, 7, 13, 17, 20 Exercise 24, 28 Case 33
3	Cost Terminology and Cost Flows	Question 2, 4, 5, 6, 8, 11, 14 Exercise 21, 22, 25, 28, 30, 36, 37 Problem 42, 44, 46, 50 Case 54
4	Including Overhead in Product and Service Costs	Question 1, 4, 8, 10, 11, 17, 22 Exercise 24, 25, 28, 31, 33, 37, 39 Problem 44, 46, 47, 49, 52, 55, 57 Case 58
	EXAM 1 – Chapters 1-4	
9	Relevant Costing	Question 1, 4, 8, 12, 17, 23, 24 Exercise 25, 28, 30, 32, 33, 36, 37 Problem 43, 46, 47, 48, 49, 50, 53 Case 55
10	Managerial Aspects of Budgeting	Question 1, 6, 11, 16, 22, 23 Exercise 24, 25, 26, 27, 30, 31 Problem 40, 41 Case 42
11	The Master Budget	Question 2, 5, 6, 7, 10, 16, 19, 20 Exercise 22, 23, 25, 28, 29, 30, 31 Problem 36, 37, 39, 40, 42, 44 Case 45
12	Controlling Noninventory Costs	Question 3, 6, 8, 10, 12, 14, 18 Exercise 19, 21, 23, 26, 29, 32 Problem 38, 40, 42, 43, 44, 47, 48 Case 49
	EXAM 2 – Chapters 9-12	

CHAPTER	TOPIC TO BE COVERED	SUGGESTED ASSIGNMENT
8	Variable Costing and Cost-Volume-Profit Analysis	Question 1, 4, 10, 15, 24 Exercise 26, 30, 34, 36, 41, 43, 48 Problem 60, 62, 64, 66, 71 Case 73
15	Responsibility Accounting and Transfer Pricing in Decentralized Operations	Question 1, 5, 6, 8, 13, 15, 18, 19 Exercise 21, 23, 24, 27, 28, 31, 34 Problem 41, 42, 43, 44, 46, 47, 50 Case 51
13	Controlling Inventory and Production Costs	Question 1, 5, 9, 12, 16, 20, 22 Exercise 23, 24, 25, 30, 31, 32, 33 Problem 42, 43, 46, 48, 49, 51 Case 52

EXAM 3 – Chapters 8, 15, 13

CHAPTER	TOPIC TO BE COVERED	SUGGESTED ASSIGNMENT
5	Activity-Based Management	Question 2, 3, 6, 9, 11, 15, 20 Exercise 21, 22, 25, 26, 30 Problem 39, 43, 44 Case 45
14	Capital Asset Selection and Capital Budgeting	Question 2, 6, 9, 13, 17, 19, 25 Exercise 28, 30, 32, 35, 38, 39, 42 Problem 50, 52, 54, 58, 59, 62, 65 Case 66
16	Measuring and Rewarding Performance	Question 1, 5, 6, 10, 14, 15, 19 Exercise 24, 28, 30, 32, 35, 36, 37 Problem 47, 48, 49, 50, 51, 53 Case 54

EXAM 4 – Chapters 5, 14, 16

Review for Final Exam

COMPREHENSIVE FINAL EXAM

TWELVE CHAPTER SYLLABUS

CHAPTER	TOPIC TO BE COVERED	SUGGESTED ASSIGNMENT
1	Management Accounting in a Global Business Environment	Question 3, 8, 13, 15 Exercise 23, 25, 27, 28 Case 38
2	Management Accounting in Quality-Oriented Environment	Question 1, 5, 7, 13, 17, 20 Exercise 24, 28 Case 33
3	Cost Terminology and Cost Flows	Question 2, 4, 5, 6, 8, 11, 14 Exercise 21, 22, 25, 28, 30, 36, 37 Problem 42, 44, 46, 50 Case 54
4	Including Overhead in Product and Service Costs	Question 1, 4, 8, 10, 11, 17, 22 Exercise 24, 25, 28, 31, 33, 37, 39 Problem 44, 46, 47, 49, 52, 55, 57 Case 58

EXAM 1 – Chapters 1-4

CHAPTER	TOPIC TO BE COVERED	SUGGESTED ASSIGNMENT
9	Relevant Costing	Question 1, 4, 8, 12, 17, 23, 24 Exercise 25, 28, 30, 32, 33, 36, 37 Problem 43, 46, 47, 48, 49, 50, 53 Case 55
10	Managerial Aspects of Budgeting	Question 1, 6, 11, 16, 22, 23 Exercise 24, 25, 26, 27, 30, 31 Problem 40, 41 Case 42
11	The Master Budget	Question 2, 5, 6, 7, 10, 16, 19, 20 Exercise 22, 23, 25, 28, 29, 30, 31 Problem 36, 37, 39, 40, 42, 44 Case 45
12	Controlling Noninventory Costs	Question 3, 6, 8, 10, 12, 14, 18 Exercise 19, 21, 23, 26, 29, 32 Problem 38, 40, 42, 43, 44, 47, 48 Case 49

EXAM 2 – Chapters 9-12

CHAPTER	TOPIC TO BE COVERED	SUGGESTED ASSIGNMENT
8	Variable Costing and Cost-Volume-Profit Analysis	Question 1, 4, 10, 15, 24 Exercise 26, 30, 34, 36, 41, 43, 48 Problem 60, 62, 64, 66, 71 Case 73
13	Controlling Inventory and Production Costs	Question 1, 5, 9, 12, 16, 20, 22 Exercise 23, 24, 25, 30, 31, 32, 33 Problem 42, 43, 46, 48, 49, 51 Case 52
5	Activity-Based Management	Question 2, 3, 6, 9, 11, 15, 20 Exercise 21, 22, 25, 26, 30 Problem 39, 43, 44 Case 45
14	Capital Asset Selection and Capital Budgeting	Question 2, 6, 9, 13, 17, 19, 25 Exercise 28, 30, 32, 35, 38, 39, 42 Problem 50, 52, 54, 58, 59, 62, 65 Case 66

EXAM 3 – Chapters 8, 13, 5, 14

Review for Final Exam

COMPREHENSIVE FINAL EXAM

MULTIPLE CHOICE QUESTIONS FROM CMA EXAMINATIONS

Chapter	Exam Date	Part	Question Number	Multiple Choice Item Number	How Used
1	NONE USED				
2	NONE USED				
3	June 1994	3	17	1	B
	June 1994	3	2	2	B
	June 1994	3	3	3	B
4	December 1993	3	15	1	B
	December 1993	4	28	2	B
	December 1990	3	2	3	B
	June 1991	3	16	4	B
	June 1991	3	17	5	B
	June 1991	3	19	6	B
5	December 1993	3	1	1	B
6	December 1994	3	23	1	B
	December 1994	3	25	2	B
	December 1994	3	28	3	B
	December 1993	3	25	4	B
	December 1993	3	24	5	B
7	December 1986	4	14	1	B
	December 1986	4	15	2	B
	December 1986	4	16	3	B
	December 1986	4	17	4	B
8	December 1973	4	1	1	B
	December 1973	4	2	2	B
	December 1990	3	29	3	B
	December 1990	3	30	4	B
	June 1993	4	1	5	B
	June 1993	4	2	6	B
	June 1993	4	3	7	B
9	June 1987	5	20	1	B
	December 1990	4	11	2	B
	December 1990	4	12	3	B
	June 1991	4	7	4	B
	June 1991	4	9	5	B
	June 1991	4	10	6	B
	June 1991	4	12	7	B
	December 1988	5	12	8	B
	December 1988	5	13	9	B
10	June 1979	4	7	1	B
	June 1991	3	7	2	B
11	December 1983	4	22	1	B
	December 1983	4	23	2	B
	December 1983	4	24	3	B
	December 1983	4	25	4	B
	June 1986	4	26	5	B
	June 1986	4	27	6	B

Chapter	Exam Date	Part	Question Number	Multiple Choice Item Number	How Used
12	June 1978	4	10	1	B
	June 1978	1	11	2	B
13	December 1983	5	22	1	B
	December 1983	5	24	2	B
	December 1985	5	12	3	B
	December 1985	5	13	4	B
	December 1985	5	15	5	B
	December 1986	5	10	6	B
	December 1986	5	11	7	B
	June 1988	5	21	8	B
	June 1988	5	23	9	B
14	December 1977	5	14	1	B
	December 1978	5	12	2	B
	December 1991	4	1	3	B
	December 1991	4	2	4	B
	December 1991	4	3	5	B
	December 1991	4	4	6	B
15	June 1989	4	25	1	B
16	June 1981	4	2	1	B

B – Both the question and answer were used. Slight modifications were made to some items.

MANAGEMENT ACCOUNTING IN A GLOBAL BUSINESS ENVIRONMENT

Learning Objectives

After reading and studying Chapter 1, you should be able to:

1. Compare financial, management, and cost accounting.

2. Explain why management accounting information is important to managers.

3. Relate management accounting to the various managerial functions.

4. Differentiate among the stages of production.

5. Distinguish between product and period costs.

6. Explain how markets have become international in scope and how this has affected the way firms compete.

7. Discuss organizational structure relationships. (Appendix)

Terminology

Authority The right (usually by virtue of position or rank) to use resources to accomplish a task or achieve an objective (From **Appendix**)

Controller The person who supervises operations of the accounting system, but does not handle or negotiate changes in actual resources (From **Appendix**)

Controlling The exerting of managerial influence on operations so that they will conform to plans

Conversion The process of changing raw materials and supplies into a different form

Decision making A process of choosing among the alternative solutions available for a particular course of action

Distribution cost Any cost incurred to fill an order for a product or service; includes all money spent on warehousing, delivering, and/or shipping products and services to customers

Dumping Selling products abroad at lower prices than those charged in the home country or in other national markets

Effectiveness The successful accomplishment of a task

Efficiency Performing tasks to produce the best outcome at the lowest cost from the resources used

Ethical standard A moral code of conduct for an individual

European Community (EC) An economic alliance originally created in 1957 as the European Economic Community by France, Germany, Italy, Belgium, the Netherlands, and Luxembourg — and later joined by the United Kingdom, Ireland, Denmark, Spain, Portugal, and Greece; has eliminated virtually all barriers to the flow of capital, labor, goods, and services among member nations; under the terms of the Maastricht Treaty (1993), the EC became the European Union

European Union (EU) See European Community

Foreign Corrupt Practices Act (FCPA) A law designed to prevent U.S. companies from offering or giving bribes (directly or indirectly) to foreign officials for the purpose of influencing those officials (or causing them to use their influence) to help the companies obtain or retain business

General Agreement on Trades and Tariffs (GATT) A treaty among many nations setting standards for trade and tariffs for signees

Goal A desired result or condition, contemplated in qualitative terms

Global economy An economy characterized by the international trade of goods and services, the international movement of labor, and international flows of capital and information

Globalization A changeover in local markets from competition among nation or local suppliers to competition among international suppliers

Grease payment A facilitating payment to a minor employee

Inventoriable cost See product cost

Line employee A person who is directly responsible for achieving an organization's goals and objectives (From **Appendix**)

Management accounting The process of identification, measurement, accumulation, analysis, preparation, interpretation, and communication of financial information used by management to plan, evaluate, and control within an organization and to assure appropriate use of and accountability for its resources

Matrix structure An organizational structure in which functional departments and project teams exist simultaneously so that the resulting lines of authority resemble a grid (From **Appendix**)

North American Free Trade Agreement (NAFTA) An agreement among Canada, Mexico, and the United States establishing the North American Free Trade Zone, with a resulting reduction in trade barriers

Objective A target that can be expressed in quantitative terms to be achieved during a preestablished period or by a specified date

Organization chart An illustration of the functions, divisions, and positions in a company and how they are related (From **Appendix**)

Overhead The indirect or supporting costs of converting materials or supplies into finished products or services

Performance evaluation Determining the degree of success in accomplishing a task; relates to both effectiveness and efficiency

Planning Translating goals and objectives into the specific activities and resources required to achieve those goals and objectives

Product cost Any cost associated with making or acquiring inventory; also called inventoriable cost

Relevant information Information that is logically related to the decision under consideration, is important to a decision maker, and has a connection to or bearing on some future endeavor; information that is useful to managers in fulfilling their organizational functions

Responsibility The obligation to accomplish a task or achieve an objective (From **Appendix**)

Staff employee A person who is responsible for providing advice, guidance, and service to line personnel (From **Appendix**)

Treasurer The person who generally handles the actual resources in an organization but who does not have access to the accounting records. (From **Appendix**)

Value chain The linked set of value-creating activities beginning with the basic raw material sources and concluding with delivery of the ultimate end-use product to the final consumer

Work in process Goods or services that have been started, but are not yet complete

Lecture Outline

A. Relationship of Financial, Management, and Cost Accounting

1. Accounting information should address the following four functions:

   a. Provide information to external parties such as ① stockholders, ② creditors, and ③ various regulatory bodies;

   b. help estimate the costs of products and services;

   c. help control operations; and

   d. help in product and service pricing.

2. Financial accounting and management accounting use a common data base in order to provide information to external and internal users, respectively.

3. Financial accounting must comply with generally accepted accounting principles (GAAP) since it focuses on external users.

   a. Financial accounting uses historical, quantifiable, monetary, and accurate information.

   b. The above characteristics are vital to the consistency, verifiability, and uniformity needed for external financial statements.

   c. Financial accounting information is normally aggregated and relates to the whole organization.

4. **Management accounting** refers to the process of identification, measurement, accumulation, analysis, preparation, interpretation, and communication of financial information used by management to plan, evaluate, and control within an organization and to assure appropriate use of and accountability for its resources.

   a. Management accounting focuses on the information needs of an organization's managers. In a business organization, information comes in various forms: ① qualitative, ② quantitative, ③ factual, and ④ estimated.

   b. Management accounting information usually focuses on the segmental characteristics of an entity.

c. Management accounting is normally not required by any organization or regulatory body.

d. Management accounting information should ① serve management's needs and ② be developed and provided only if the cost of producing the information is less than the benefit derived from using the information.

5. **Cost accounting** is an area of management accounting that focuses on determining the cost of making products or performing services.

a. Cost accounting is a mutually shared subset of both financial and management accounting and cost accounting information creates an overlap between financial accounting and management accounting. (See text **Exhibit 1-3**)

b. Cost accounting interfaces with financial accounting by providing product cost measurements for inventories and cost of goods sold on the financial statements.

c. Cost accounting – as part of management accounting – provides part of the quantitative cost-based information needed by management to ① assess product profitability, ② prepare budgets, and ③ make decisions concerning investments.

6. Information, in order to be useful to managers, must be relevant. Relevant information satisfies the following three conditions:

a. Relevant information is logically related to the decision being considered;

b. it is important to the decision maker; and

c. it has a connection to or a bearing on some future endeavor.

B. **Management Functions**

1. **Goals** are desired results or conditions contemplated in qualitative terms.

2. **Objectives** are targets expressed in quantitative terms that can be achieved during a preestablished period or by a specified date. Objectives should logically result from goals.

3. **Planning** is the translating of goals and objectives into the specific activities and resources required to achieve those goals and objectives.

   a. Companies develop short-term, intermediate-term, and long-term plans.

   b. Short-term plans are prepared in more detail than are intermediate-term or long-term plans and are used by managers as one basis for the control and performance evaluation functions.

4. **Controlling** is the exerting of managerial influence on operations so that they will conform to plans.

   a. The control process uses norms or standards against which actual results are compared.

   b. Controlling involves setting performance standards, measuring performance, periodically comparing actual performance with standards, and taking corrective action when operations do not conform with established standards.

5. **Performance evaluations** determine the degree of success in accomplishing a task; equates to both effectiveness and efficiency.

   a. Performance evaluations can be utilized by managers, using management accounting information, to determine if operations are proceeding according to plan or if actual results differ significantly from those that were expected.

   b. Adjustments to operating activities may be needed if actual results differ significantly from those that were expected.

   c. Effectiveness is the successful accomplishment of a task.

   d. Efficiency is performing tasks to produce the best outcome at the lowest cost from the resources used.

6. **Decision making** is a process of choosing among the alternative solutions available for a particular course of action. A manager's ability to manage depends on good decision making.

   a. Managers are the information users while accountants are the information providers.

  b. The quantity of information needed by managers is related both to the expected consequences of the decision and the complexity of activities performed by the organization.

  c. More information is desired and needed by managers currently than in the past due to the various ways in which business is changing.

  d. The world has essentially become smaller due to the development of technology.

C. **Stages of Production** (See text **Exhibit 1-4**)

  1. The processing of a product or the performance of a service flows through three stages:

  a. Pre-production or work not started (raw materials and supplies);

  b. work in process; and

  c. finished work.

  2. The total accumulated production costs for materials, labor, and overhead equal the cost of goods in the third state (finished work).

  3. The primary accounts involved in the cost accumulation process are:

  a. Raw Materials Inventory and/or Supplies,

  b. Work in Process Inventory, and

  c. Finished Goods Inventory.

  4. Service firms do not usually have the same degree of cost complexity as do manufacturing firms.

  a. Supplies are inventoried in the work not started stage until they are placed into a work in process stage, where labor and overhead are added to achieve finished results.

  b. Conversion costs may be accumulated for work in process, but an inventory of finished is not usually maintained.

  5. A **value chain** is the linked set of value-creating activities beginning with the basic raw material sources and concluding with delivery of the ultimate end-use product to the final consumer.

D. **Product costs and Period Costs** (See text **Exhibits 1-6** and **1-7**)

    1. A **product cost** is any cost associated with making or acquiring inventory; also called an inventoriable cost – while all other costs are called **period costs**.

    2. Product costs for a merchandising form are relatively easy to determine and the only significant product cost is the purchase cost.

    3. Manufacturing and service companies execute numerous value chain activities and the costs of the activities must be accumulated and assigned to the outputs as product costs.

        a. Manufacturers, in order to maintain control over the production process, must account for ① raw materials and supplies, ② work in process for partially processed goods, and ③ finished goods inventory.

        b. Each type of inventory requires its own account.

        c. Product costs for services are expensed on the income statement in a *Cost of Services Rendered* account since services are not usually warehoused.

    4. Period costs are noninventoriable and are related to time periods.

        a. A period cost is any cost other than one associated with making or acquiring inventory.

        b. Period costs are related to other business operations, like the selling and administrative areas.

        c. Period costs are more closely associated with a particular time frame rather than with the production or acquisition of a product or the performance of a service.

        d. A **distribution cost** is a cost incurred to warehouse, transport, or deliver a product or service. Even though distribution costs are expensed as incurred (like many other period costs), managers cannot lose sight of the fact that these costs relate directly to products and services.

E. The Global Environment of Business

1. **Globalization** of markets involves a changeover in local markets from competition among nation or local suppliers to competition among international suppliers.

   a. The **global economy** represents an economy characterized by the international trade of goods and services, the international movement of labor, and international flows of capital and information.

   b. Globalization has created marketing opportunities for goods and services as well as new vendor sources for production inputs.

   c. Globalization creates for any business two major decision areas – ① a business strategy must be devised that considers both domestic as well as international competitors, and ② the company must be cognizant of conditions in various markets around the world in order to identify markets in which the company has both the strengths and the desire to compete.

2. A global business strategy must be carefully planned.

   a. Businesses often discover that the easiest way to precipitate a presence in foreign markets is to acquire an existing business that serves those markets, but differences in international accounting practices can cause problems in the global merger market.

   b. Companies need to know that operating in foreign markets can generate some risks not found in domestic markets.

3. Legal and ethical considerations are important since courts are holding companies responsible for both product and process quality.

   a. Legal and ethical standards vary from one country to another.

   b. Government is heavily involved in regulating business activities, especially in the United States, and such regulation is becoming more concerned with issues other than those controlling pricing and profitability.

   c. More laws are now being written to assure ① fair disclosure of corporate information to third parties, ② protection of consumers, and ③ the safeguarding of natural resources.

d. All firms in the United States are subject to filing periodic reports with the IRS (Internal Revenue Service), large corporations whose stock is publicly traded are required to furnish periodic financial reports to the SEC (Securities and Exchange Commission), and many companies must file similar reports to both state and foreign governments.

e. Product and environmental liability are two major areas of legal consideration.

f. **The Foreign Corrupt Practices Act** (FCPA) is a law passed by Congress in 1977 that makes it illegal for a company to engage in various "questionable" foreign payments and makes it mandatory for a company to maintain accurate accounting records and a reasonable system of internal control.

g. **Grease payments** are facilitating payments to minor employees such as custom officials to expedite the processing of goods on the dock and are excluded from the FCPA.

h. **Ethical standards** are moral codes of conduct for individuals and are not as formally acknowledged in society as are laws.

4. Trade agreements between countries that reduce fiscal and physical barriers to trade have become commonplace in order to promote a global economy in the 1990s.

a. The **European Community** (EC) is an economic alliance originally created in 1957 as the European Economic Community by France, Germany, Italy, Belgium, the Netherlands, and Luxembourg – and later joined by the United Kingdom, Ireland, Denmark, Spain, Portugal, and Greece.

b. The EC has eliminated virtually all barriers to the flow of capital, labor, goods, and services among member nations.

c. The EC became the **European Union** under the terms of the Maastricht Treaty (1993).

d. The **North American Free Trade Agreement (NAFTA)** is an agreement among Canada, Mexico, and the United States establishing the North American Free Trade Zone, with a resulting reduction in trade barriers.

e. The **General Agreement on Trades and Tariffs (GATT)** is a treaty among many nations setting standards for trade and tariffs for signees.

f. **Dumping** refers to the selling of products abroad at lower prices than those charged in the home country or in other national markets.

F. Organizational Structure – Appendix

1. An organization is a system comprised of humans, nonhuman resources, and commitments configured to achieve certain explicit and implicit goals and objectives.

2. An **organization chart** is a depiction of the functions, divisions, and positions of the people/jobs in a company and how they are related; indicates the lines of authority and responsibility in an organization. (See text **Exhibit 1-10**)

   a. A **line employee** is an employee who is directly responsible for achieving an organization's goals and objectives.

   b. A staff employee is an employee who is responsible for providing advice, guidance, and service to line personnel.

3. The organization chart also indicates the lines of authority and responsibility.

   a. **Authority** is the right (usually by virtue of position or rank) to use resources to accomplish a task or achieve an objective.

   b. **Responsibility** is the obligation to accomplish a task or achieve an objective. While authority can be delegated or assigned to others, ultimate responsibility cannot be delegated.

4. The **grapevine** includes the informal relationships and channels of communication that exist in an organization.

5. The **treasurer** is an individual (in a corporation) who handles the actual resources of the organization but who does not have access to the accounting records.

6. The **controller** is the chief accountant (in a corporation) who is responsible
   for maintaining and reporting on both the cost and financial sets of
   accounts but who does not handle or negotiate changes in actual resources.

7. A **matrix structure** is an organizational structure in which functional
   departments and project teams exist simultaneously so that the resulting
   lines of authority resemble a grid.

MANAGEMENT ACCOUNTING IN QUALITY-ORIENTED ENVIRONMENT

Learning Objectives

After reading and studying Chapter 2, you should be able to:

1. Discuss how companies are addressing the demand for product and service quality.

2. Explain the underlying factors supporting the concept of total quality management.

3. Differentiate between process and results benchmarking.

4. Discuss how a company's move along the quality continuum could be assessed.

5. Identify and discuss recent changes in technology that are affecting current business practices.

6. Discuss why a strategically based management accounting system is needed in addition to a financial accounting system.

Terminology

Baldrige Award An award program administered by the U.S. Department of Commerce to recognize quality achievements by U.S. businesses

Bar codes Groups of lines and spaces arranged in a special machine-readable pattern

Benchmarking The process of investigating, comparing, and evaluating the company's products, processes, and/or services against those of companies believed to be the "best in class" so the investigating company can imitate and possibly improve on their techniques

Continuous improvement Small but ongoing efforts to make positive adjustments in the status quo

Control chart A graphical presentation of the results of a specified activity; indicates the upper and lower control limits and those results that are out of control

Customer A generic term for the recipient or beneficiary of a process's output; can be internal or external

Cycle time The time from when a customer places an order to the time that product or service is delivered or, using a full life-cycle approach, the time from the conceptualization of a product or service to the time the product or service is delivered to the customer

Decentralization The downward delegation by top management of authority and decision making to the individuals who are closest to internal processes and customers

Deming Prize Japan's premier quality award

Design for manufacturability The process of reducing the number of parts in a product, using standard (rather than special order) parts when possible, and simplifying the assembly process

Electronic data interchange (EDI) The almost instantaneous computer-to-computer transfer of information

Empowerment All practices that are designed to give workers the training and authority they need to manage their own jobs

Flexible manufacturing system (FMS) A production system in which a single factory manufactures numerous variations on products through the use of computer-controlled robots

Innovation Dramatic improvements in the status quo caused by radical new ideas, technological breakthroughs, or large investments in new technology or equipment

ISO 9000 A set of standards established by the international community to define the minimum acceptable quality for processes that generate products and services offered in international trade

Just-in-time (JIT) A philosophy about when to do something; the *when* is "as needed" and the *something* is a production, purchasing, or delivery activity

Malcolm Baldrige Quality Award See Baldrige Award

Process benchmarking Benchmarking in which the quality of internal processes are assessed by comparing them with similar processes of firms identified as having the highest quality processes globally; also involves subsequent efforts to emulate and improve on the quality achievements of the benchmark firms

Quality circle An intra- or interdepartmental team of empowered workers who meet to identify and solve quality-related problems

Results benchmarking Benchmarking in which an end product or service is examined; the focus is on product/service specifications and performance results

Strategic cost management (SCM) The managerial use of cost information for the purpose(s) of setting and communicating organizational strategies; establishing, implementing, and monitoring the success of methods to accomplish the strategies; and assessing the level of success in meeting the promulgated strategies

Total quality management (TQM) A philosophy for organizational management and organizational change that seeks ever-increasing quality

Lecture Outline

A. The Demand for Quality

1. **Total quality management (TQM)** is a philosophy for organizational management and organizational change that seeks ever-increasing quality.

   a. **Continuous improvement** refers to small but ongoing efforts to make positive adjustments in the status quo.

   b. The objective of TQM is continuous improvement and the underlying principles are ① customer focus, ② process improvement, and ③ total organizational involvement.

   c. Management is responsible for providing employees with the necessary resources to support the achievement of this objective and these principles. (See text **Exhibit 2-1**)

   d. A company striving for TQM must have all of its employees perceive continuous improvement as a routine part of the work environment: It must become a way of life.

   e. **Innovation** involves dramatic improvements in the status quo caused by radical new ideas, technological breakthroughs, or large investments in new technology or equipment.

2. Customer focus is important since customer expectations, which have been designated as the ultimate arbiters of quality in a TQM approach to business, continue to rise.

   a. **Customer** is a generic term for the recipient or beneficiary of a process's output; can be internal or external. (See text **Exhibit 2-2**)

   b. A company must determine who its value-adding customers are and then must understand what those customers want.

   c. A firm has to monitor its customers and their needs because ① external customers' needs change during the product or service life and ② customer needs and expectations rise as a product or product group matures.

   d. Companies that implement TQM must also consider and adequately service their internal customers.

e. **Decentralization** refers to the downward delegation by top management of authority and decision making to the individuals who are closest to internal processes and customers.

f. **Empowerment** refers to all practices that are designed to give workers the training and authority they need to manage their own jobs. (See text **Exhibit 2-3**)

g. Empowered employees must, for empowerment to be effective: ① understand how their jobs fit into the "big picture;" ② recognize the needs of their customers; ③ have the knowledge, skills, and resources to properly perform their jobs; ④ be educated to make appropriate judgments; ⑤ be held responsible for the outcomes of their decisions; and ⑥ believe that they are trusted by and can trust management.

h. **Quality circles** are intra- or interdepartmental teams of empowered workers who meet to identify and solve quality-related problems.

3. Process improvement and benchmarking allow companies to identify and devote more time to processes that have poor value-to-cost relationships.

a. **Control charts** are graphical presentations of the results of specified activities; indicate the upper and lower control limits and those results that are out of control.

b. Workers can seek to make significant, practical improvements once processes have been defined, standardized, and stabilized.

c. **Benchmarking** is the process of investigating, comparing, and evaluating the company's products, processes, and/or services against those of companies believed to be the "best in class" so the investigating company can imitate and possibly improve on their techniques.

d. **Process benchmarking** is benchmarking in which the quality of internal processes are assessed by comparing them with similar processes of firms identified as having the highest quality processes globally; also involves subsequent efforts to emulate and improve on the quality achievements of the benchmark firms.

e. **Results benchmarking** refers to benchmarking in which an end product or service is examined; the focus is on product/service specifications and performance results.

4. Quality awards are earned by companies internationally.

  a. The **Baldrige Award** (Malcolm Baldrige Quality Award) is an award program administered by the U.S. Department of Commerce to recognize quality achievements by U.S. businesses and was established by the 1987 Malcolm Baldrige National Quality Improvement Act as the embodiment of TQM in the United States. (See text **Exhibit 2-6**)

  b. The **Deming Prize** is Japan's premier quality award and is named for W. Edwards Deming.

  c. The **ISO 9000** is a set of standards established by the international community to define the minimum acceptable quality for processes that generate products and services offered in international trade that was developed in 1987 by the International Organization for Standardization based in Geneva, Switzerland. (See text **Exhibit 2-7**)

5. Total employee involvement at all levels is essential for TQM to be successfully implemented.

  a. Committed and consistent top management leadership is the driving force for moving the company culture toward an *esprit de corps* in which every individual feels compelled to meet and even surpass customer expectations.

  b. Top management has to ① be involved in the quality process, ② develop and sustain an environment that is conducive to quality improvements, and ③ set an example of commitment to TQM. (See text **Exhibit 2-8**)

  c. A management information system for planning, controlling, and decision making must exist.

  d. Companies move along a quality continuum in order to achieve world-class status. (See text **Exhibit 2-9**)

B. **The Need for Reduced Cycle Time**

1. **Cycle time** may be viewed as the time from when a customer places an order to the time that product or service is delivered or, using a full life-cycle approach, the time from the conceptualization of a product or service to the time the product or service is delivered to the customer.

2. Companies strive to reduce cycle time for at least three major reasons.

    a. Reduction of cycle time allows companies to react more quickly to customer requirements and, therefore, are engaging in a TQM focus.

    b. Reduction in cycle time allows companies to bring products to market more rapidly and, therefore, be more competitive.

    c. Cycle time reduction creates a need to reduce waste in all processes.

3. **Design for manufacturability** refers to the process of reducing the number of parts in a product, using standard (rather than special order) parts when possible, and simplifying the assembly process.

4. **Just-in-time (JIT)** is a philosophy about when to do something; the *when* is "as needed" and the *something* is a production, purchasing, or delivery activity.

    a. The JIT philosophy is applicable to all departments of every type of organization and has three primary goals: ① elimination of any production process or operation that does not add value to the product/service; ② continuous improvement in production/performance efficiency; and ③ reduction in the total cost of production/performance while increasing quality.

    b. A firm with a JIT inventory system does not make or buy a product until a customer demands it, and the JIT system is dependent upon the accuracy of market data since a tight linkage is necessary between sales and production volume.

    c. High-quality production processes are mandatory in order to avoid defects.

    d. JIT production promotes ① flexibility in production processes, ② short lead times, ③ short production runs, ④ quick setups, ⑤ and greatly reduced inventory levels.

    e. Cycle time reduction necessitates that all business functions (design, development, production, ordering, shipping, and billing) be accelerated.

    f. Continuous improvement efforts will gradually reduce cycle time, but innovation (which is usually caused by technology) is needed in order to make substantial rapid reductions in cycle time.

C. Increased Technological Abilities

1. The firm possessing the highest level of technology *and* the employees with the skill to employ that technology to its utmost generally finds itself a step ahead of the competition.

2. Companies have now entered what can be called the Information Revolution and new information technologies are becoming progressively less expensive and, at the same time, increasingly more powerful.

   a. Technological innovations have dramatically advanced accounting and other information systems, and even small companies have computerized their accounting, customer, and supplier records.

   b. Investments in technology may be necessary for the sake of systems integration; as new technology is developed, this systems integration trend is likely to accelerate.

3. **Electronic data interchange (EDI)** refers to the almost instantaneous computer-to-computer transfer of information.

   a. EDI systems allow firms to eliminate paperwork and electronically communicate with their customers and suppliers.

   b. Electronic communication lessons the likelihood of errors in communication and reduces the preparation and sending time for written communication through conventional methods like the postal services, and eliminates manual data entries that would otherwise be required to update inventory and related accounting records.

4. Each product or service in a customer-focused manufacturing environment should be defect-free.

   a. A point of inception for this objective is the requirement that all material inputs and conversion processes be essentially flawless.

   b. Major determinants in aiding an organization in its attainment of total quality are: ① employee empowerment and training, ② strong supplier relationships, and ③ technologically advanced production equipment.

   c. **Bar codes** are groups of lines and spaces arranged in a special machine-readable pattern which have revolutionized retailing.

d. Bar coding is the most visible of numerous manufacturing technologies; computerized technology is utilized in modern manufacturing equipment to schedule, control, and monitor production with limited or no human intervention.

e. Computer programs in highly integrated systems oversee each production process and develop statistical data on both the process and component reliability; production defects should be readily discovered and corrected due to this concentrated oversight process.

f. Poka-yoke, meaning "mistake proofing," is the term used in Japan to describe such techniques.

5. A **flexible manufacturing system (FMS)** is a production system in which a single factory manufactures numerous variations on products through the use of computer-controlled robots.

a. Flexible manufacturing systems require a high level of investment in equipment and in research and development; also, increased product variety causes manufacturers to incur substantial overhead costs for the stocking and ordering of components.

b. Consumers' perceptions of the value-to-price relationship for a firm's products and services will be reflected in the firm's success in a global, quality-based competitive environment.

D. **Strategy-Based Cost Management Practices**

1. **Strategic cost management (SCM)** can be viewed as the managerial use of cost information for the purpose(s) of setting and communicating organizational strategies; establishing, implementing, and monitoring the success of methods to accomplish the strategies; and assessing the level of success in meeting the promulgated strategies.

2. Cost accumulation and process measurement activities must be considered in designing a management accounting system under SCM.

3. A strategically based cost management system would provide a way to distinguish costs that add value from those that do not so that managers and employees could work to reduce such costs.

4. A strategically based management accounting system would report a greater number of the costs and benefits of organizational activities for management's decision-making needs.

COST TERMINOLOGY
AND COST FLOWS

Learning Objectives

After reading and studying Chapter 3, you should be able to:

1. Understand the assumptions accountants make about cost behavior and why these assumptions are necessary.

2. Understand the relationship between cost objects and direct costs.

3. Recognize how the conversion process works in manufacturing and service companies.

4. Classify product costs into direct materials, direct labor, and factory overhead categories.

5. Calculate cost of goods manufactured.

Terminology

Allocate Assign based on the use of a cost predictor or an arbitrary method

Appraisal cost A quality control cost incurred for monitoring or inspection; compensates for mistakes not eliminated through prevention

Conversion cost The sum of direct labor and factory overhead costs; the cost incurred in changing direct materials or supplies into finished products or services

Cost A monetary measure of the resources given up to acquire a good or a service

Cost behavior The manner in which a cost responds to a change in a related level of activity

Cost driver A factor that has a direct cause-effect relationship to a cost

Cost object Anything to which costs attach or are related

Cost of goods manufactured (CGM) The total cost of the goods that were completed and transferred to Finished Goods Inventory during the period

Direct cost A cost that is clearly, conveniently, and economically traceable to a particular cost object

Direct labor The time spent by individuals who work specifically on manufacturing a product or performing a service and whose efforts are conveniently and economically traceable to that product or service

Direct material A readily identifiable, physical part of a product that is conveniently and economically traceable to that product

Failure cost A quality control cost associated with goods or services that have been found not to conform or perform in accordance with the required standards, as well as all related costs (such as that of the complaint department); may be internal or external

Fixed cost A cost that remains constant in total within a specified range of activity

Indirect cost A cost that cannot be clearly traced to a particular cost object; a common cost

Mixed cost A cost that has both a variable and a fixed component; it does not fluctuate in direct proportion to changes in activity, nor does it remain constant with changes in activity

Outsource Using a source external to the company to provide a service or manufacture a needed product or component

Predictor An activity measure that changes in a consistent, observable manner with changes in another item

Prevention cost A quality control cost incurred to improve quality by preventing defects from occurring

Prime cost The sum of direct materials costs and direct labor costs

Relevant range The specified range of activity over which a variable cost remains constant per unit or a fixed cost remains fixed in total

Step cost A variable or fixed cost that shifts upward or downward when activity changes by a certain interval or step

Variable cost A cost that varies in total in direct proportion to changes in activity

Lecture Outline

A. **Cost** is a frequently-used word and reflects a monetary measure of the resources given up to acquire a good or a service.

B. **Cost Classification Categories** – Cost Classifications and Types of Costs (See text **Exhibit 3-1**)

C. **Cost Behavior**

   1. The **relevant range** is the specified range of activity over which a variable cost remains constant per unit or a fixed cost remains fixed in total.

   2. A **cost driver** is an activity or occurrence that has a direct cause-effect relationship with a cost.

   3. A **predictor** is an activity measure that changes in a consistent, observable manner with changes in another item.

   4. Variable and fixed are the two most common types of cost behaviors.

      a. A **variable cost** is a cost that varies in total in direct proportion to changes in activity.

      b. A **fixed cost** is a cost that remains constant in total within a specified range of activity.

      c. **Outsource** means using a source external to the company to provide a service or manufacture a needed product or component.

   5. Mixed and step are two other common types of cost behaviors.

      a. A **mixed cost** is a cost that has both a variable and a fixed component; it does not fluctuate in direct proportion to changes in activity, nor does it remain constant with changes in activity.

      b. A **Step cost** is a variable or fixed cost that shifts upward or downward when activity changes by a certain interval or step: ① step variable costs have small steps and ② step fixed costs have large steps.

D. **Components of Product Cost**

   1. A **cost object** is anything to which costs attach or are related.

2. A **direct cost** is a cost that is clearly, conveniently, and economically traceable to a particular cost object.

3. An **indirect cost** is a cost that cannot be clearly traced to a particular cost object; a common cost.

4. A **direct material** is a readily identifiable, physical part of a product that is conveniently and economically traceable to that product.

5. **Direct labor** refers to the time spent by individuals who work specifically on manufacturing a product or performing a service and whose efforts are conveniently and economically traceable to that product or service.

6. **Factory Overhead** is any factory or production cost that is indirect to the product or service; does not include direct materials or direct labor.

7. **Quality costs** are a category of overhead costs.

   a. **Prevention costs** are quality control costs incurred to improve quality by preventing defects from occurring.

   b. **Appraisal costs** are quality control costs incurred for monitoring or inspection; compensates for mistakes not eliminated through prevention.

   c. **Failure costs** are quality control costs that are associated with goods or services that have been found not to conform or perform in accordance with the required standards, as well as all related costs (such as that of the complaint department); may be internal or external.

8. **Prime cost** is the sum of direct materials costs and direct labor costs.

9. **Conversion cost** is the sum of direct labor and factory overhead costs; the cost incurred in changing direct materials or supplies into finished products or services.

E. **Accumulation of Product Costs**

1. Periodic inventory system

2. Perpetual inventory system – all product costs flow through Work in Process Inventory to Finished Goods Inventory and, ultimately, to Cost of Goods Sold (see text **Exhibit 3-12**).

F. **Cost of Goods Manufactured and Sold** (see text **Exhibit 3-13**)

   1. Schedule of Cost of Goods Manufactured

   2. Schedule of Cost of Goods Sold

G. **Income Statement Comparisons – Appendix**

   1. A merchandising company has only one inventory account and, thus, Cost of Goods Sold reflects only changes within the Merchandise Inventory account.

   2. A manufacturing organization has three inventory accounts.

     a. The Cost of Goods Sold section of its Income Statement depicts the changes in Finished Goods Inventory.

     b. A manufacturer supports its Cost of Goods Sold computation with a Schedule of Cost of Goods Manufactured for the period.

   3. A service company computes the Cost of Services Rendered instead of Cost of Goods Sold.

Multiple Choice Questions from CMA Examinations

1. An example of an internal failure cost is
   a. maintenance.
   b. inspection.
   c. rework.
   d. product recalls.
   e. cusomer losses.

   The correct answer is c. (CMA June 1994, 3-17)

2. In cost terminology, prime costs consist of
   a. direct materials and variable factory overhead.
   b. direct labor and indirect labor.
   c. indirect labor and fixed factory overhead.
   d. direct labor and direct materials.
   e. direct labor and variable factory overhead.

   The correct answer is d. (CMA June 1994, 3-2)

3. In cost terminology, conversion costs consist of
   a. direct and indirect labor.
   b. direct labor and direct materials.
   c. direct labor and factory overhead.
   d. indirect labor and variable factory overhead.
   e. Prime costs and and fixed factory overhead.

   The correct answer is c. (CMA June 1994, 3-3)

INCLUDING OVERHEAD IN PRODUCT AND SERVICE COSTS

Learning Objectives

After reading and studying Chapter 4, you should be able to:

1. Distinguish among the various systems and methods of product costing.

2. Discuss how predetermined factory overhead rates overcome the deficiencies of applying actual factory overhead to production.

3. Analyze mixed costs using the high-low method and (Appendix 1) least-squares regression analysis.

4. Explain the usefulness of flexible budgeting to managers.

5. Develop predetermined factory overhead rates and understand how the selection of a capacity measure affects factory overhead application.

6. Account for underapplied or overapplied factory overhead at yearend and discuss why these accounting techniques are appropriate.

7. Understand why separate predetermined overhead rates are generally more useful than combined rates.

8. (Appendix 2) Allocate service department costs to revenue-producing departments using the direct and step methods.

Terminology

Actual cost system A method of accumulating product or service costs that uses actual direct materials, actual direct labor, and actual overhead costs

Administrative department An organizational unit that performs management activities that benefit the entire organization (from **Appendix 2**)

Applied overhead The amount of overhead assigned to Work in Process Inventory as a result of the occurrence of the activity that was used to develop the application rate; the result of multiplying the quantity of actual activity by the predetermined rate

Benefits-provided ranking A listing of service departments in an order that begins with the one providing the most service to all other organizational areas; the ranking ends with the service department that provides the least service to all but the revenue-producing areas (from **Appendix 2**)

Capacity A measure of production volume or of some other cost driver related to plant production capability during a period

Correlation A statistical measure of the strength of relationship between two variables

Cost pool A grouping of all costs that are associated with the same activity or cost driver

Dependent variable An unknown variable that is to be predicted by use of one or more independent variables

Direct method (of service department cost allocation) A method that uses a specific base to assign service department costs directly to revenue-producing departments with no intermediate cost allocations (from **Appendix 2**)

Employee time sheet (time ticket) A source document that indicates, for each employee, what jobs were worked on during the day and for what amount of time

Expected activity A short-run concept representing the anticipated level of activity for the upcoming year

Flexible budget A series of financial plans that detail the individual variable and fixed cost factors comprising total cost and present those costs at different levels of activity according to cost behavior

High-low method A technique for separating mixed costs that uses actual observations of a total cost at the highest and lowest levels of activity and calculates the change in both activity and cost; the levels chosen must be within the relevant range

Independent variable A variable that, when changed, will cause consistent, observable changes in another variable; a variable used as the basis of predicting the value of a dependent variable

Job A single unit or group of like units identifiable as being produced to distinct customer specifications

Job order costing The product costing system used by entities that produce tailor-made goods or services in limited quantities that conform to specifications designated by the purchaser of those goods or services

Job order cost sheet A source document that provides virtually all the financial information about a particular job; the set of all job order cost sheets for uncompleted jobs composes the Work in Process Inventory subsidiary ledger

Least-squares regression analysis A statistical technique for mathematically determining the cost line of a mixed cost that best fits the data set by considering all representative data points; allows the user to investigate the relationship between or among dependent and independent variables (from **Appendix 1**)

Materials requisition A source document that indicates the types and quantities of materials to be placed into production or used in performing a service; causes materials and their costs to be released from the raw materials warehouse and sent to Work in Process Inventory

Normal capacity A firm's long-run average activity (over five to ten years) which gives effect to historical and estimated future production levels and to cyclical and seasonal fluctuations

Normal cost system A method of accumulating product or service costs that uses actual direct materials and direct labor costs but assigns overhead costs to Work in Process Inventory through the use of a predetermined overhead rate

Outlier A nonrepresentative point that either falls outside the relevant range or is a distortion of typical cost-volume relationships within the relevant range

Overapplied overhead Overhead applied to Work in Process Inventory that is greater than actual overhead incurred for a period

Practical capacity The activity level that could be achieved during normal working hours given unused capacity and ongoing, regular operating interruptions, such as holidays, downtime, and start-up time

Predetermined overhead rate A budgeted constant charge per unit of activity used to assign overhead costs to production or services

Process costing system The product costing system used by entities that produce large quantities of homogeneous goods in continuous mass production

Regression line A line that represents the cost formula for a set of cost observations fit to those observations in a mathematically determined manner (from **Appendix 1**)

Service department An organizational unit that performs one or more specific functional support or assistance tasks for other internal units (from **Appendix 2**)

Simple regression A method in which only one independent variable is used to predict a dependent variable in least-squares regression (from **Appendix 1**)

Standard A benchmark or norm against which actual results may be compared

Standard cost system A system in which budgeted costs for direct materials, direct labor, and/or factory overhead are used to account for manufacturing a single unit of product or performing a single service; the budgeted costs represent the ideal predetermined expenditures that should be incurred to achieve a specific objective

Step method (of service department cost allocation) A method in which service department costs are assigned to cost objects by the use of a specific base after the most important interrelationships of the service departments and the revenue-producing departments have been considered (from **Appendix 2**)

Theoretical capacity The estimated absolute maximum potential production activity that could occur in a production facility during a specific time frame

Underapplied overhead Overhead applied to Work in Process Inventory that is less than actual overhead

Variance Any difference between an actual and an expected cost

Lecture Outline

A. **Methods of Product Costing**

   1. Products can be costed after a determination is made about:

      a. the type of product system and

      b. the method of measurement to be used. (See text **Exhibit 4-1**)

   2. Job order costing and process costing are the two basic costing systems

      a. **Job order costing** is the product costing system used by entities that produce tailor-made goods or services in limited quantities that conform to specifications designated by the purchaser of those goods or services.

      b. **Process costing** is the product costing system used by entities that produce large quantities of homogenous goods in continuous mass production. Process costing systems use either the weighted average or FIFO cost flow assumption. (See text **Chapter 7**)

   3. The three basic **measurement methods** are: (1) actual, (2) normal, and (3) standard costing.

      a. An **actual cost system** constitutes a method of accumulating product or service costs that uses actual direct materials, actual direct labor, and actual overhead costs.

      b. A **predetermined overhead rate** is an average constant budgeted constant charge per unit of activity used to assign overhead costs to production or services.

      c. A **normal cost system** is a method of accumulating product or service costs that uses actual direct materials and direct labor costs but assigns overhead costs to Work in Process Inventory through the use of a predetermined overhead rate.

      d. **Standards** are benchmarks or norms against which actual results may be compared.

e. **Standard cost system** a system in which budgeted costs for direct materials, direct labor, and/or factory overhead are used to account for manufacturing a single unit of product or performing a single service; the budgeted costs represent the ideal predetermined expenditures that should be incurred to achieve a specific objective

B. **Job Order Costing**

1. Costs are accumulated individually by job in a job order product costing system.

   a. Costs of different jobs are maintained in separate subsidiary ledger accounts and are not added together or commingled in those ledger accounts.

   b. Direct materials, direct labor, and factory overhead are accumulated for each job.

   c. Actual, normal, or standard costing can be used in a job order costing environment.

2. The output of a given job can be a single unit or multiple similar or dissimilar units.

3. A **materials requisition** is a source document that indicates the types and quantities of materials to be placed into production or used in performing a service; causes materials and their costs to be released from the raw materials warehouse and sent to Work in Process Inventory.

4. A **job order cost sheet** is a source document that provides virtually all the financial information about a particular job; the set of all job order cost sheets for uncompleted jobs composes the Work in Process Inventory subsidiary ledger.

5. An **employee time sheet (time ticket)** is a source document that indicates, for each employee, what jobs were worked on during the day and for what amount of time.

C. Predetermined Overhead Rates

1. A **predetermined overhead rate** is a budgeted constant charge per unit of activity used to assign overhead costs to production or services.

   a. The overhead rate is calculated by dividing total estimated annual overhead cost by a related estimated measure of volume or activity, or cost driver, in advance of the year of application.

   b. The rate may be either a departmental or a plantwide rate.

3. Three reasons for using predetermined overhead rates rather than actual overhead costs:

   a. A predetermined overhead rate allows overhead to be assigned to the goods produced or services rendered during the period rather than at the end of the period.

   b. Predetermined overhead rates can compensate for fluctuations in actual overhead costs that have nothing to do with activity levels.

   c. Predetermined overhead rates can overcome the problem of fluctuations in activity levels that have no impact on actual fixed overhead costs.

4. Separate predetermined overhead rates should be developed for the variable and fixed elements of overhead cost because variable and fixed overhead costs behave differently.

D. Analyzing Mixed Costs

1. Mixed costs contain both a variable and a fixed cost element and are assumed by accountants to be linear rather than curvilinear.

2. The **high-low method** of analyzing mixed costs is a technique for separating mixed costs that uses actual observations of a total cost at the highest and lowest levels of activity and calculates the change in both activity and cost; the levels chosen must be within the relevant range of activity.

   a. The method uses the highest and lowest observed levels of actual activity to determine the change in costs which reflects the variable cost element.

   b. The fixed portion of a mixed cost is found by subtracting total variable cost from total cost.

   c. An **independent variable** is a variable that, when changed, will cause consistent, observable changes in another variable; a variable used as the basis of predicting the value of a dependent variable.

   d. A **dependent variable** is an unknown variable that is to be predicted by use of one or more independent variables.

   e. **Outliers** are abnormal or nonrepresentative points that either fall outside the relevant range or are distortions of the typical cost-volume relationships within the relevant range.

3. The **least squares regression analysis** is a method of analyzing mixed costs (**Appendix 1**)

4. **Correlation** is a statistical measure of the strength of relationship between two variables.

E. **Preparing Flexible Budgets** (See text **Exhibits 4-4 and 4-5**)

1. A **flexible budget** is a series of financial plans that detail the individual variable and fixed cost factors comprising total cost and present those costs at different levels of activity according to cost behavior.

2. A flexible budget presents variable and fixed costs at various levels of activity within a relevant range of activity.

3. Flexible budgets are prepared for both product and period costs.

F. **Developing and Using Predetermined Overhead Rates**

1. **Variable overhead** changes in total proportionately with some measure of volume or activity and includes indirect materials, hourly-paid indirect labor, and the variable component of any mixed cost.

   a. Individual predetermined overhead rates should be calculated for each variable overhead component, and all individual rates totaled to find the overall predetermined variable overhead rate.

   b. Variable overhead per unit is assumed to remain constant at any level of activity within the relevant range, so that the activity level chosen to estimate total cost is not relevant.

c. The rate is used to apply overhead to Work in Process Inventory based on the actual magnitude of the activity base.

d. Predetermined overhead calculations are always made prior to the year of application.

e. **Variances** are any differences between an actual and an expected cost.

6. **Fixed overhead** is that component of total overhead that remains constant in total as activity changes within the relevant range.

a. Fixed overhead per unit varies inversely in response to changes in activity.

b. A particular level of activity must be specified to compute the predetermined fixed overhead rate per unit of activity. Such a specified activity level is normally the company's expected annual capacity.

7. **Capacity** refers to a measure of production volume or some other cost driver related to plant production capability during a period.

a. **Theoretical capacity** is the estimated absolute maximum potential production activity that could occur in a production facility during a specific time frame.

b. **Practical capacity** is the activity level that could be achieved during normal working hours given unused capacity and ongoing, regular operating interruptions, such as holidays, downtime, and start-up time.

c. **Normal capacity** is a firm's long-run average activity (over five to ten years) which gives effect to historical and estimated future production levels and to cyclical and seasonal fluctuations.

d. **Expected activity (expected annual capacity)** is a short-run concept representing the anticipated level of activity for the upcoming year.

G. **Overhead Application**

1. **Applied overhead** is the amount of overhead assigned to Work in Process Inventory as a result of the occurrence of the activity that was used to develop the application rate; the result of multiplying the quantity of actual activity by the predetermined rate.

2. Actual overhead incurred during a period will rarely equal applied overhead; this difference represents underapplied or overapplied overhead.

   a. **Underapplied overhead** is the amount of overhead applied to Work in Process Inventory that is less than actual overhead.

   b. **Overapplied overhead** is the amount of overhead applied to Work in Process Inventory that is greater than actual overhead incurred for a period.

3. Disposition of underapplied or overapplied overhead is recorded annually.

   a. The method of disposition of underapplied or overapplied overhead depends upon the materiality of the amount involved.

   b. The amount is closed to Cost of Goods Sold if it is immaterial.

   c. The amount, if it is material, should be allocated among the accounts containing applied overhead: ① Work in Process Inventory, ② Finished Goods Inventory, and ③ Cost of Goods Sold.

H. **Combined Overhead Rates**

1. Combined overhead rates are traditional in businesses for three reasons: (1) clerical ease, (2) clerical cost savings, and (3) absence of any formal requirement to separate overhead costs by cost behavior.

2. Information may become more and more distorted as the degree of combination increases from combining related cost pools to combining all factory overhead.

3. Product cost more clearly reflects the different amounts and types of machine or labor work performed on the products if departmental overhead rates are used.

4. The true cost of the product may be distorted, selling prices might be set too high or too low, causing management to make incorrect decisions if plant-wide overhead rates, rather than departmental rates, are used.

I. **Least-Squares Regression Analysis – Appendix 1**

1. **Least squares regression analysis** is a statistical technique for mathematically determining the cost line of a mixed cost that best fits the data set by considering all representative data points; allows the user to investigate the relationship between or among dependent and independent variables. (See text **Exhibit 4-9**)

2. **Outliers** may be inadvertently used in the application of the high-low method.

3. Least squares regression analysis helps to select the independent variable that is the best predictor of the dependent variable when multiple independent variables exist.

4. **Simple regression** analysis is a method in which only one independent variable is used to predict a dependent variable in least-squares regression.

5. A **regression line** is a line that represents the cost formula for a set of cost observations fit to those observations in a mathematically determined manner.

G. **Allocation of Service Department Costs – Appendix 2**

1. **Service departments** are organizational units that perform one or more specific functional support or assistance tasks for other internal units.

   a. **Administrative departments** are organizational units that perform management activities that benefit the entire organization.

   b. Costs of service and administrative departments are referred to collectively as "service department costs."

   c. Non-revenue-producing activities are conducted merely to support revenue-producing activities.

   d. Service department costs are often allocated to revenue-producing user departments.

2. Rational and systematic allocation bases should reflect consideration of four criteria in determining the appropriate allocation base:

    a. the benefits received by the revenue-producing department from the service department;

    b. a cause-and-effect relationship between factors in the revenue-producing department and costs incurred in the service department;

    c. the fairness of the service department allocations between or among revenue-producing departments; and

    d. the ability of revenue-producing departments to bear the allocated costs.

3. Three basic allocation methods are used to allocate the pooled service department costs to the revenue-producing departments.

    a. The **direct method** is a method that uses a specific base to assign service department costs directly to revenue-producing departments with no intermediate cost allocations.

    b. The **step method** is a method in which service department costs are assigned to cost objects by the use of a specific base after considering the most important interrelationships of the service departments and the revenue-producing departments. The "benefits-provided" ranking is utilized to allocate the costs. A **benefits-provided ranking** is a listing of service departments in an order that begins with the one providing the most service to all other organizational areas; the ranking ends with the service department that provides the least service to all but the revenue-producing areas.

4. The final step in allocating service department costs is the determination of the overhead application rates for the revenue-producing departments, regardless of the method used. (See text **Exhibits 4-10 and 4-11**)

Multiple Choice Questions from CMA Examinations

1. Multiple or departmental overhead rates are considered preferable to a single or plant-wide overhead rate when

   a. manufacturing is limited to a single product flowing through identical departments in a fixed sequence.
   b. various products are manufactured that do not pass through the same departments or use the same manufacturing techniques.
   c. cost drivers, such as direct labor, are the same over all processes.
   d. individual cost drivers cannot accurately be determined with respect to cause-and-effect relationships.
   e. the single or plant-wide rate is related to several identified cost drivers.

   The correct answer is b. (CMA December 1993, 3-15)

2. Regression analysis
   a. estimates the independent cost variable.
   b. uses probability assumptions to determine total project costs.
   c. estimates the dependent cost variable.
   d. ignores the coefficient of determination.
   e. encompasses factors outside the relevant range.

   The correct answer is c. (CMA December 1993, 4-28)

3. Allocation of service department costs to the production departments is necessary to:
   a. control costs.
   b. coordinate production activity.
   c. determine overhead rates.
   d. maximize efficiency.
   e. measure use of plant capacity.

   The correct answer is c. (CMA December 1990, 3-2)

Questions 4 through 6 are based on the following information. The managers of Rochester Manufacturing are discussing ways to allocate the cost of service departments such as Quality Control and Maintenance to the production departments. To aid them in this discussion, the controller has provided the following information:

	Quality Control	Maintenance	Machining	Assembly	Total
Budgeted overhead costs before allocation	$350,000	$200,000	$400,000	$300,000	$1,250,000
Budgeted machine hours	–	–	50,000	–	50,000
Budgeted direct labor hours	–	–	–	25,000	25,000
Budgeted hours of service:					
Quality control	–	7,000	21,000	7,000	35,000
Maintenance	10,000	–	18,000	12,000	40,000

4. If Rochester Manufacturing uses the direct method of allocating service department costs, the total service costs allocated to the assembly department would be:

a. $ 80,000.

b. $ 87,500.

c. $120,000.

d. $167,500.

e. $467,500.

The correct answer is d. (CMA June 1991, 3-16)

5. Using the direct method, the total amount of overhead allocated to each machine hour at Rochester Manufacturing would be:

a. $ 2.40.

b. $ 5.25.

c. $ 8.00.

d. $ 9.35.

e. $15.65.

The correct answer is e. (CMA June 1991, 3-17)

6. If Rochester Manufacturing uses the step-down method of allocating service department costs beginning with quality control, the maintenance costs allocated to the assembly department would be:

a. $ 70,000.
b. $108,000.
c. $162,000.
d. $200,000.
e. $210,000.

The correct answer is b. (CMA June 1991, 3-19)

Solution

Direct Method:

Relative distribution of services:

From/To	Quality Control	Maintenance	Machining	Assembly
Quality Control			75.00%	25.00%
Maintenance			60.00%	40.00%

Distribution of costs:

From/To	Quality Control	Maintenance	Machining	Assembly
Costs	$ 350,000	$ 200,000	$ 400,000	$ 300,000
Allocation:				
Quality Control	(350,000)		262,500	87,500
Maintenance		(200,000)	120,000	80,000
Totals	(350,000)	(200,000)	382,500	167,500
Total costs	$ 0	$ 0	$ 782,500	$467,500
			50,000	
				25,000
			$ 15.65	$ 18.70

Step-down Method:

Relative distribution of services:

From/To	Quality Control	Maintenance	Machining	Assembly
Quality Control		20.00%	60.00%	20.00%
Maintenance			60.00%	40.00%

Distribution of costs:

From/To	Quality Control	Maintenance	Machining	Assembly
Costs	$ 350,000	$ 200,000	$ 400,000	$ 300,000
Allocation:				
Quality Control	(350,000)	70,000	210,000	70,000
Maintenance		(270,000)	162,000	108,000
Totals	(350,000)	(200,000)	372,000	178,000
Total costs	$ 0	$ 0	$ 772,000	$478,000
			50,000	
				25,000
			$ 15.44	$ 19.12

ACTIVITY-BASED MANAGEMENT

Learning Objectives

After reading and studying Chapter 5, you should be able to:

1. Discuss how reasonably accurate product and service cost information can be developed.

2. Differentiate between and provide examples of value-added and non-value-added activities.

3. Identify the causes of decreased manufacturing cycle efficiency.

4. Designate the cost drivers in an activity-based costing system.

5. Distinguish between activity-based costing and conventional overhead allocation methods.

6. Determine when the use of activity-based costing is appropriate.

7. Recognize the benefits and limitations of using activity-based costing.

Terminology

Activity A repetitive action, movement, or work sequence performed to fulfill a business function

Activity-based costing (ABC) An accounting information system that identifies the various activities performed in an organization and collects costs on the basis of the underlying nature and extent of those activities

Activity-based management (ABM) A discipline that focuses on how the activities performed during the production/performance process can improve the value received by a customer and the profit achieved by providing this value

Activity center A segment of the production or service process for which management wants a separate report of the costs of activities performed

Activity driver A measure of the demands placed on activities and, thus, the resources consumed by products and services; often indicates an activity's output

Batch-level cost A cost that is created by a group of similar things made, handled, or processed at a single time

Business process reengineering (BPR) Process innovation and redesign aimed at finding and implementing radical changes in how things are made or how tasks are performed to achieve substantial cost, service, or time reductions

Business-value-added activity An activity that is necessary for the operation of a business but for which a customer would not want to pay

Facility-level cost See organization-level cost

Idle time Storage time and time spent waiting at a production operation for processing

Inspection time The time taken to perform quality control

Long-term variable cost A cost that has traditionally been viewed as fixed, but which will actually react to some significant change in activity; a step fixed cost

Manufacturing cycle efficiency (MCE) Value-added production time divided by total cycle time; provides a measure of processing efficiency

Mass customization Relatively low-cost mass production of products to the unique specifications of individual customers; requires the use of flexible manufacturing systems

Non-value-added activity (NVA) An activity that increases the time spent on a product or service but does not increase its worth

Organization-level cost A cost incurred to support ongoing operations to provide available facilities

Pareto principle Rule stating that the greatest effects in human endeavors are traceable to a small number of causes (the *vital few*), while the majority of causes (the trivial many) collectively yield only a small impact; this relationship is often referred to as the 20-80 rule

Process map A flowchart or diagram that indicates every step in making a product or providing a service

Processing time The time it takes to perform the functions necessary to manufacture a product

Process-level cost A cost created by the need to implement or support a specific process

Product complexity The number of components in a product or the number of processes or operations through which a product flows

Product-level cost A cost that is caused by the development, production, or acquisition of a type of product

Product variety The number of different types of products produced

Service time The time it takes to perform all necessary service functions for a customer

Simultaneous (concurrent) engineering An integrated approach in which all primary functions and personnel contributing to a product's origination and production are involved continuously for the beginning of a project

Transfer time The time it takes to move products or components from one place to another (move time)

Unit-level cost A cost created by the production or acquisition of a single unit of product or the delivery of a single unit of service

Value-added activity (VA) An activity that increases the worth of a product or service to the customer and for which the customer is willing to pay

Value chart A visual representation of the value-added and non-value-added activities and the time spent in all of these activities from the beginning to the end of a process

Lecture Outline

A. **Developing Product/Service Cost Information**

1. Product or service costs are developed for three purposes:

   a. to have information that enables management to report to stockholders and various regulatory bodies;

   b. to help management make product decisions such as pricing and product line expansions or deletions; and

   c. to allow management to monitor and control operations.

2. The modern manufacturing environment is highly machine-intensive, with high overhead costs and low direct labor costs.

   a. The use of direct labor hours as the overhead allocation base in such an atmosphere can cause serious product cost distortions since most overhead costs in these environments are machine-related.

   b. Incurrence of overhead is not solely related to machine hours, however; it is often related to product variety, product complexity, or other cost drivers.

   c. Such an environment requires more sophisticated measures of overhead cost allocation.

B. **Activity Analysis**

1. Product or service cost development, although specifically designated as an accounting function, is a major concern of all managers.

2. **Activity-based management (ABM)** is a discipline that focuses on how the activities performed during the production/performance process can improve the value received by a customer and the profit achieved by providing this value. (See text **Exhibit 5-1**)

   a. An **activity** is a repetitive action, movement, or work sequence performed to fulfill a business function.

   b. A **process map** is a flowchart or diagram that indicates every step in making a product or providing a service.

3. Activities may be designated as value-added and non-value-added activities.

   a. A **value chart** is a visual representation of the value-added and non-value-added activities and the time spent in all of these activities from the beginning to the end of a process.

   b. A **value-added activity (VA)** is an activity that increases the worth of a product or service to the customer and for which the customer is willing to pay.

   c. A **non-value-added activity (NVA)** is an activity that increases the time spent on a product or service but does not increase its worth.

   d. A **business-value-added activity** is an activity that is necessary for the operation of a business but for which a customer would not want to pay.

4. Time spent executing NVA activities can be classified as ① NVA production or performance time, ② inspection time, ③ transfer time, and ④ idle time.

   a. The time taken to perform quality control is **inspection time**.

   b. The time it takes to move products or components from one place to another is **transfer time** (move time).

   c. Storage time and time spent waiting at a production operation for processing is **idle time**.

5. Value-added production time divided by total cycle time is **manufacturing cycle efficiency □ (MCE)**.

6. **Just-in-time (JIT)** refers to the idea that inventory is manufactured or purchased only as the need for it arises or in time to be sold or used. Its use eliminates a significant portion of the idle time consumed in the storage and wait processes. (see text **Chapter 2**)

7. The accounting system must recognize that costs are created and incurred because their drivers occur at different levels in order to reflect more complex environments. (see text **Exhibit 5-3**)

   a. Costs have traditionally been accumulated into one or two cost pools — **total factory overhead** or **variable** and **fixed factory overhead**, either by departments or on a plant-wide basis.

b. One or two cost drivers — **direct labor hours** and/or **machine hours** — have been used to assign costs to products.

·c. The use of single cost pools and single cost drivers may produce illogical product or service costs in complex production (or service) environments.

d. A **unit-level cost** is a cost created by the production or acquisition of a single unit of product or the delivery of a single unit of service.

8. An activity-based system recognizes that costs may vary at levels of activity "higher" than the unit level, and such higher levels include batch, product or process, and organizational or facility levels. (see text **Exhibit 5-5**)

a. A **batch-level cost** is a cost that is created by a group of similar things made, handled, or processed at a single time.

b. A **product-level cost** is a cost that is caused by the development, production, or acquisition of a type of product

c. A **process-level cost** is a cost created by the need to implement or support a specific process.

d. An **organizational-level cost** is a cost incurred to support ongoing operations to provide available facilities.

C. **Activity-Based Costing (ABC)**

1. **ABC** is an accounting information system that identifies the various activities performed in an organization and collects costs on the basis of the underlying nature and extent of those activities.

2. An **activity center** is a segment of the production or service process for which management wants a separate report of the costs of activities performed. (see text **Exhibit 5-7**)

a. Costs, after being initially recorded, are accumulated in activity center cost pools using first-step cost drivers that reflect the appropriate level of cost incurrence (unit, batch, or product/process).

b. Gathering costs in pools reflecting the same cost drivers allows managers to recognize any cross-functional activities in an organization.

c. Costs are allocated out of the activity center cost pools and assigned to products and services by use of a second-step driver, referred to as an activity driver.

3. An **activity driver** is a measure of the demands placed on activities and, thus, the resources consumed by products and services; often indicates an activity's output.

4. ABC is illustrated in text **Exhibit 5-8**.

D. **Determining if ABC is Appropriate**

1. ABC is a useful tool, but is not necessarily appropriate for all companies, and certain factors must be considered when deciding whether or not to implement ABC.

2. Two cost drivers that cause long-term variable costs to change are product variety and product complexity.

   a. **Product variety** refers to the number of different types of products produced.

   b. The **Pareto principle** is a rule stating that the greatest effects in human endeavors are traceable to a small number of causes (the *vital few*), while the majority of causes (the trivial many) collectively yield only a small impact; this relationship is often referred to as the 20-80 rule.

   c. **Product complexity** refers to the number of components in a product or the number of processes or operations through which a product flows.

3. **Simultaneous (concurrent) engineering** is an integrated approach in which all primary functions and personnel contributing to a product's origination and production are involved continuously from the beginning of a project.

4. **Business process reengineering (BPR)** constitutes process innovation and redesign aimed at finding and implementing radical changes in how things are made or how tasks are performed to achieve substantial cost, service, or time reductions.

5. Companies now have a greater ability technologically to implement ABC than in the past.

E. **Operational Control under ABC**

1. Most companies use activity-based costing in a stand-alone fashion, separate from their conventional cost accounting systems – although some companies have partially integrated ABC with their conventional systems. (see text **Exhibit 5-11**)

2. Activity-based costing is often employed to improve performance and enhance management's ability to make better product profitability analyses, and should not be perceived as a substitute or alternative for conventional systems, but a means by which to provide additional, more accurate information.

3. Traditional accounting systems concentrate on controlling cost incurrence, while ABC focuses on controlling the source of the cost incurrence.

4. ABC systems indicate that significant resources are consumed by low-volume products and complex production operations.

F. **Criticisms of and Conclusions about ABC** (see text **Exhibit 5-11**)

1. ABC implementation necessitates a considerable amount of time and cost. Significant support is needed throughout the firm for the implementation process to be successful.

2. ABC does not specifically comply with generally accepted accounting principles.

3. Companies desiring to implement ABC systems must be aware that, while more accurate costing may be provided, ABC systems are not always appropriate.

4. Another criticism that has been charged is that ABC does not, in and of itself, promote total quality management and continuous improvement. However, companies can implement ABC and its related management techniques in support of and in conjunction with TQM, JIT, and any other world-class methodologies.

Multiple Choice Questions from CMA Examinations

1. Cost drivers are
    a. activities that cause costs to increase as the activity increases.
    b. accounting techniques used to control costs.
    c. accounting measurements used to evaluate whether or not performance is proceeding according to plan.
    d. a mechanical basis, such as machine hours, computer time, size of equipment, or square footage of factory, used to assign costs to activities.
    e. Costs linked to two or more other costs.

The correct answer is a. (CMA December 1993, 3-1)

INTRODUCTION TO A STANDARD COST SYSTEM

Learning Objectives

After reading and studying Chapter 6, you should be able to:

1. Understand how standards for material and labor are set.

2. Explain why standard cost systems are used.

3. Calculate materials, labor, and overhead variances.

4. Analyze variances for purposes of control and performance evaluation.

5. Recognize how organizational evolution and desired level of attainability affect standard setting.

6. Understand how standard setting and standard usage are changing in modern business.

7. (Appendix) Prepare journal entries for a standard cost system.

Terminology

Bill of materials A document that contains information about product material components, their specifications (including quality), and the quantities needed for production

Cost table Data base that provides information about how using different input resources, manufacturing processes, and product designs will affect product costs

Expected standard A standard that reflects what is actually expected to occur in a future period

Fixed overhead spending variance The difference between actual and budgeted fixed overhead

Kaizen costing Continuous efforts to reduce product costs, improve product quality, and/or improve the production process after manufacturing activities have begun

Labor efficiency variance (LEV) The difference between the number of actual direct labor hours worked and the standard hours allowed for the actual output multiplied by the standard labor rate per hour

Labor rate variance (LRV) The difference between the total actual direct labor wages for the period and the standard rate for all hours actually worked during the period

Management by exception A technique in which managers set upper and lower limits of tolerance for deviations and investigate only deviations that fall outside those tolerance ranges

Material price variance (MPV) The amount of money spent below (F for favorable) or above (U for unfavorable) the standard price for a given quantity of materials; may be calculated for quantity purchased or quantity used

Material quantity variance (MQV) The cost saved (F for favorable) or expended (U for unfavorable) because of the difference between the actual quantity of material used and the standard quantity of material allowed for the goods produced during the period

Operations flow (or routing) document A listing of all tasks necessary to make a unit of product or perform a service and the time allowed for each operation

Practical standard A standard that allows for normal, unavoidable time problems or delays, such as machine downtime and worker breaks; can be reached or slightly exceeded approximately sixty to seventy percent of the time with reasonable effort by workers

Price variance The difference between what was paid and what should have been paid for inputs during the period

Quantity variance The difference between the quantity of actual inputs and the standard quantity of inputs for the actual output of the period multiplied by a standard price or rate

Standard cost A budgeted or estimated cost to manufacture a single unit of product or perform a single service

Standard cost card A document that summarizes the direct material and direct labor standard quantities and prices needed to complete one unit of product as well as the overhead allocation bases and rates

Standard quantity allowed A measure of quantity that translates the actual output achieved into the standard input quantity that should have been used to achieve that output

Target costing A Japanese method of determining the maximum allowable cost of a product before it is designed, engineered, or produced by subtracting an acceptable profit margin rate from a forecasted selling price

Theoretical standard A standard that allows for no inefficiency of any type and is, therefore, sometimes called a perfection or an ideal standard

Total variance The difference between total actual cost incurred and total standard cost applied for the output produced during the period; can also be designated by cost components (direct materials, direct labor, variable factory overhead, and fixed factory overhead)

Variable overhead efficiency variance The difference between budgeted variable overhead at actual input activity and budgeted variable overhead at standard input activity allowed

Variable overhead spending variance The difference between actual variable overhead and budgeted variable overhead based on actual input

Variance Any difference between actual and standard costs or quantities

Variance analysis The process of categorizing the nature (favorable or unfavorable) of the differences between standard and actual costs and seeking the reasons for those differences

Volume variance The difference between budgeted and applied fixed overhead

Lecture Outline

A. Standard Cost Systems

1. Standards are benchmarks or norms against which actual results may be compared.

2. Standards can also be used for motivation and control purposes.

3. A **variance** is any difference between actual and standard costs or quantities.

B. Development of a Standard Cost System

1. **Target costing** is a Japanese method of determining the maximum allowable cost of a product before it is designed, engineered, or produced by subtracting an acceptable profit margin rate from a forecasted selling price. (See text **Exhibit 6-1**)

2. The implied maximum or target cost is compared to the expected product cost. If the target cost is less than the expected cost, the company has several alternatives.

   a. The product design and/or production process can be changed to reduce costs. **Cost tables** are databases that provide information about the effects on product costs of using different input resources, manufacturing processes, and product designs; they help in determining how such adjustments can be made.

   b. A less-than-desired profit margin can be accepted.

   c. The company can decide that it does not want to enter this particular product market at the current time because it cannot make the profit margin it desires.

3. **Kaizen costing** involves continuous efforts to reduce product costs, improve product quality, and/or improve the production process after manufacturing activities have begun. (See text **Exhibit 6-2**)

4. Standards are conventionally established for each component (materials, labor, and overhead) of product cost.

  a. A **standard cost** is a budgeted or estimated cost to manufacture a single unit of product or perform a single service.

  b. The development of a standard cost involves judgment and practicality in identifying the types of material and labor to be used and their related quantities and prices.

  c. The development of standards for overhead requires that costs are appropriately classified by cost behavior, valid allocation bases have been chosen, and a reasonable level of activity has been specified.

5. Standards should be developed by a group, composed of representatives from the following areas: (1) management accounting, (2) product design, (3) industrial engineering, (4) personnel, (5) data processing, (6) purchasing, and (7) management.

C. Material Standards

1. The first step in developing material standards is to identify and list the specific direct material components used to manufacture the product or to perform the service.

2. Three things must be known about the materials: (1) what inputs are needed; (2) what the quality of those inputs must be; and (3) what quantities of inputs of the specified quality are needed.

3. Physical quantity estimates can be made in terms of weight, size, volume, or other measures — given the level of quality chosen for each essential component.

4. The estimates should be based on the results of engineering tests, opinions of people using the materials, or historical data.

5. The bill of materials is a document that contains information about product material components, their specifications (including quality), and the quantities needed for production. (see text **Exhibit 6-3**)

D. Labor Standards

1. The development of labor standards requires the same basic procedures as those used for materials.

2. An analysis of labor tasks is completed, then an **operations flow (or routing) document** can be prepared which lists all tasks necessary to make a unit of product or perform a service and the corresponding time allowed for each operation. (see text **Exhibit 6-4**)

E. **Overhead Standards** are simply the predetermined overhead application rates previously discussed (see text **Chapter 4**).

1. The development of the bill of materials, operations flow document, and standard overhead costs is followed by the preparation of a standard cost card.

2. A **standard cost card** is a document that summarizes the direct material and direct labor standard quantities and prices needed to complete one unit of product as well as the overhead allocation bases and rates.

F. **Variance Computations**

1. A **total variance** is the difference between total actual cost incurred and total standard cost applied for the output produced during the period.

   a. A total variance can also be designated by cost components (direct materials, direct labor, variable factory overhead, and fixed factory overhead).

   b. Total variances indicate differences between actual and expected production costs, but they do not provide useful information for determining why such differences occurred.

2. Total variances for materials and labor are subdivided into price and quantity variances in order to help managers in their control objectives. (see text **Exhibit 6-6**)

   a. A **price variance** reflects the difference between what was paid and what should have been paid for inputs during the period.

   b. A **quantity variance** provides a monetary measure of the difference between the quantity of actual inputs and the standard quantity of inputs for the actual output of the period multiplied by a standard price or rate.

3. The **standard quantity allowed** is a measure of quantity that translates the actual output achieved into the standard input quantity that should have been used to achieve that output.

4. The total material usage variance can be subdivided into the material price variance and the material quantity variance.

   a. The **material price variance (MPV)** indicates the amount of money spent below (F for favorable) or above (U for unfavorable) the standard price for a given quantity of materials; may be calculated for quantity purchased or quantity used.

   b. The **material purchase price variance** is the materials price variance when calculated based on the quantity of materials purchased during the period rather than the quantity of materials used.

   c. The **material price usage variance** is the materials price variance when calculated based on the quantity of materials used during the period, and is commonly known as the materials price usage variance.

   d. The **material quantity variance (MQV)** indicates the cost saved (F for favorable) or expended (U for unfavorable) because of the difference between the actual quantity of material used and the standard quantity of material allowed for the goods produced during the period.

5. The total labor variance can be subdivided into the labor rate variance and the labor efficiency variance.

   a. The **labor rate variance (LRV)** shows the difference between the total actual direct labor wages for the period and the standard rate for all hours actually worked during the period.

   b. The **labor efficiency variance (LEV)** is the difference between the number of actual direct labor hours worked and the standard hours allowed for the actual output times the standard labor rate per hour.

G. **Factory Overhead Variances**

1. The use of separate variable and fixed overhead application rates and accounts allows the computation of separate variances for each type of overhead.

2. The total variable and total fixed factory overhead variances can be subdivided into specific price and quantity subvariances for each type of overhead, and are referred to as follows:

a. Variable Overhead Price Element → Variable Overhead Spending Variance

b. Variable Overhead Quantity Element → Variable Overhead Efficiency Variance

c. Fixed Overhead Price Element → Fixed Overhead Spending Variance

d. Fixed Overhead Quantity Element → Fixed Overhead Volume Variance

3. The total variable overhead (VOH) variance is the difference between actual VOH cost incurred for the period and standard variable overhead cost applied to the period's actual production or service output.

a. The **variable overhead spending variance** is the difference between actual VOH and budgeted VOH based on actual input.

b. The **variable overhead efficiency variance** is the difference between budgeted VOH at actual input activity and budgeted VOH at standard input allowed.

4. The total fixed overhead (FOH) variance is the difference between actual FOH cost incurred and standard FOH cost applied to the period's actual production.

a. The **fixed overhead spending variance** is the difference between actual and budgeted fixed overhead.

b. The fixed overhead **volume variance** is the difference between budgeted and applied fixed overhead.

H. **Cost Control and Variance Responsibility**

1. Cost control focuses on the variances between actual costs incurred for a period and the standard costs that should have been incurred based on actual output.

a. Managers must be provided with detailed information on the various cost components in order to exercise any type of control.

b. A well-designed system of cost control and variance analysis should capture variances as early as possible.

2. **Variance analysis** is the process of categorizing the nature (favorable or unfavorable) of the differences between standard and actual costs and seeking the reasons for those differences.

    a. The cost control and variance analysis system should help managers determine who or what is responsible for the variance and who is best able to explain it.

    b. An early measurement system may allow operational performance to be improved when variances reflect poor performance.

    c. The cause of a variance is more difficult to determine the longer the reporting of the variance is delayed.

    d. Material price and labor rate variances are not as controllable at the production or service level as are material quantity and labor efficiency variances.

3. Material variances can be determined at the point of purchase and at the point of issuance or usage.

    a. Material price variances are normally determined at the point of purchase, but can also be determined at the point of issuance or usage. Purchasing agents cannot always *control* prices but, given adequate lead time and resources, these individuals should be able to *influence* those prices.

    b. Material quantity variances can be determined when materials are issued or used. Such variances are considered the responsibility of the person in charge of the job or department.

4. Labor rate and efficiency variances are usually identified as a part of the payroll process and assigned to the person in charge of the service or production area, assuming that those managers have the ability to influence the type of labor personnel used.

    a. A common factor may influence both materials and labor, causing both a material variance and a labor variance.

    b. The probability of detecting relationships among variances is improved, but not assured, by timely variance reporting.

5. The difference between actual and applied overhead is the amount of underapplied or overapplied overhead or the total overhead variance that must be explained.

6. Control purposes differ for variable and fixed overhead due to the types of costs that make up the two categories as well as the ability of managers to influence those costs.

7. VOH costs are incurred on a continuing basis as work is performed and are directly related to that work.

   a. VOH is controlled by ① keeping actual costs in line with planned costs for the actual level of activity and ② getting the planned output yield from the overhead resources placed into production.

   b. VOH spending variances are normally caused by price differences – paying higher or lower average actual prices than the standard prices allowed. Such fluctuations often occur because price changes have not been reflected in the standard rate.

   c. The VOH efficiency variance reflects the managerial control implemented or needed in regard to yield of output as related to input.

8. Control of fixed overhead is different from that of variable overhead since fixed overhead may not necessarily be directly related to current activity. Control of many fixed overhead costs must occur at the time of commitment rather than at the time of activity.

   a. The fixed overhead spending variance usually represents a weighted average price variance of the components of fixed overhead, but it can also reflect the mismanagement of resources.

   b. A total fixed overhead spending variance amount would not provide management with enough specific information to decide whether corrective action would be possible or desirable.

   c. Individual cost variances for each component need to be reviewed in order to assist managers in determining the actual cause(s) of and responsibility for the various components of the total fixed overhead spending variance.

   d. The volume variance is a direct function of the capacity level chosen for the computation of the standard fixed overhead application rate.

e. The volume variance is the one variance over which managers have the least influence and control, especially in the short-run.

f. A volume variance that is unfavorable indicates utilization of capacity that is less than expected.

I. **Conversion Cost as an Element in Standard Costing** (see text **Exhibit 6-9**)

1. Direct labor cost usually represents an extremely small part of total product cost in highly automated factories.

   a. One worker typically oversees a large number of machines and is therefore heavily involved with trouble-shooting machinery malfunctions.

   b. The worker's wages might be more closely related to indirect labor than to direct labor.

2. Many companies have responded to overhead costs being so much larger than direct labor costs by adapting their standard cost systems to provide for only two elements of product cost – direct materials and conversion.

   a. Conversion costs are likely to be separated into their variable and fixed components.

   b. Conversion costs are also likely to be separated into direct and indirect categories based on their ability to be traced to a machine rather than to a product.

3. Variance analysis for conversion cost in automated plants usually focuses on (1) spending variances for overhead costs, (2) efficiency variances for machinery and production costs rather than labor costs, and (3) the traditional (more control-focused) volume variance for production.

J. **Considerations in Establishing Standards**

1. Appropriateness and attainability need to be considered when standards are established.

2. Appropriateness, in relation to a standard, refers to the basis on which the standards are developed and how long they are expected to last.

   a. Standards are developed from past and current information, and they should reflect technical and environmental factors expected for the period in which the standards are to be applied.

   b. Factors such as materials quality, normal ordering quantities, employee wage rates, degree of plant automation, facility layout, and mix of employee skills should be considered.

   c. Standards must evolve over the organization's life to reflect its changing methods and processes.

3. Attainability refers to management's belief about the degree of difficulty or rigor that should be incurred in achieving the standard. Standards can be classified by their degree of rigor and, thus, their motivational value from easy to difficult as follows: expected, practical, and ideal.

   a. **Expected standards** reflect what is actually expected to occur in a future period.

   b. **Practical standards** allow for normal, unavoidable time problems or delays, such as machine downtime and worker breaks; can be reached or slightly exceeded approximately sixty to seventy percent of the time with reasonable effort by workers.

   c. **Theoretical standards** allow for no inefficiency of any type and are, therefore, sometimes called perfection or ideal standards.

4. **Management by exception** is a technique in which mangers set upper and lower limits of tolerance for deviations and investigate only deviations that fall outside those tolerance ranges.

   a. Variances large enough to fall outside the ranges of acceptability are usually indicative of trouble, and the variances themselves do not reveal the cause of the trouble or the person or group responsible.

   c. Managers must investigate problems through observation, inspection, and inquiry to determine the causes of variances.

K. **Changes in the Use of Standards**

   1. Performance can be evaluated once ability to control can be assigned.

2. Many accountants now believe that incorrect measurements are sometimes used in utilizing variances for performance evaluation.

3. The Japanese philosophy is a notable exception to the disbelief in the use of theoretical standards for performance evaluation.

   a. The just-in-time (JIT) production systems and total quality management (TQM) concepts developed by the Japanese were started from the premises of ① zero defects, ② zero inefficiency, and ③ zero downtime.

   b. Theoretical standards become expected standards under such a system, and there is no level of acceptable deviation from those standards.

   c. The authors of the text expect that the level of attainability for standards will move away from the practical and much closer to the ideal in order for American companies to compete in global markets.

4. A point-of-purchase material price variance calculation allows managers to see the impact of buying decisions more quickly; such information may not be highly relevant in a JIT environment.

   a. A point-of-purchase price variance may impair a manager's ability to recognize a relationship between a favorable material price variance and an unfavorable material quantity variance.

   b. The effects of a purchase will not be known until the materials are actually used if a favorable price variance results from lower quality materials being purchased.

5. Company management needs to consider the incorporation of rapid changes in the environment into the standards during a year in which *significant* changes occur.

   a. Management can either ① ignore the changes or ② reflect the changes in the standard.

   b. Management may consider combining the two choices in the accounting system – ① plans prepared by use of original and new standards can be compared and ② any variances will reflect changes in the business environment.

L. **Standard Cost System Journal Entries – Appendix** (See text **Exhibit 6-10**)

Multiple Choice Questions from CMA Examinations

1. The **best** basis upon which cost standards should be set to measure controllable production inefficiencies is
   a. engineering standards based on ideal performance.
   b. normal capacity.
   c. recent average historical performance.
   d. engineering standards based on attainable performance.
   e. practical capacity.

   The correct answer is d. (CMA December 1994, 3-23)

2. An unfavorable direct labor efficiency variance could be caused by a(n)
   a. unfavorable variable overhead spending variance.
   b. unfavorable material quantity variance.
   c. unfavorable fixed overhead volume variance.
   d. favorable variable overhead spending variance.
   e. favorable fixed overhead volume variance.

   The correct answer is b. (CMA December 1994, 3-25)

3. Water Control Inc. manufacturers water pumps and uses a standard cost system. The standard factory overhead costs per water pump are based on direct labor hours and are shown below:

Variable overhead (4 hours at $8/hour)	$ 32
Fixed overhead (4 hours at $5*/hour)	20
Total overhead cost per unit	$ 52

   * Based on a capacity of 100,000 direct labor hours per month.

   The following additional information is available for the month of November.

   • 22,000 pumps were produced although 25,000 had been scheduled for production.
   • 94,000 direct labor hours were worked at a total cost of $940,000.
   • The standard direct labor rate is $9 per hour.
   • The standard direct labor time per unit is four hours.
   • Variable overhead costs were $740,000.
   • Fixed overhead costs were $540,000.

The variable overhead efficiency variance for November was
a. $ 48,000 unfavorable.
b. $ 60,000 favorable.
c. $ 96,000 favorable.
d. $200,000 unfavorable.
e. $ 32,000 favorable.

The correct answer is a. (CMA December 1994, 3-28)

Solution

Variable Overhead:

Actual VOH	**AH X SR** 94,000 X $8	**SH X SR** 88,000 x $8
$740,000	$752,000	$704,000

$12,000 F $48,000 U

VOH Spending Variance   VOH Efficiency Variance

$36,000 U

Total VOH Variance

4. A manufacturing firm planned to manufacture and sell 100,000 units of product during the year at a variable cost per unit of $4.00 and a fixed cost per unit of $2.00. The firm fell short of its goal and only manufactured 80,000 units at a total incurred cost of $515,000. The firm's manufacturing cost variance was
a. $85,000 favorable.
b. $35,000 unfavorable.
c. $ 5,000 favorable.
d. $ 5,000 unfavorable.
e. $80,000 unfavorable.

The correct answer is c. (CMA December 1993, 3-25)

Solution

Budgeted manufacturing cost ((80,000 X $4) + (100,000 X $2))	$ 520,000
Less actual manufacturing cost	515,000
Favorable manufacturing cost variance	$ 5,000

5. ChemKing uses a standard costing system in the manufacture of its single product. The 35,000 units of raw material in inventory were purchased for $105,000, and two units of raw material are required to produce one unit of final product. In November, the company produced 12,000 units of product. The standard allowed for material was $60,000, and there was an unfavorable quantity variance of $2,500.

The material price variance for the units used in November was

a. $ 2,500 unfavorable.
b. $11,000 unfavorable.
c. $12,500 unfavorable.
d. $ 3,500 unfavorable.
e. $ 2,500 favorable.

The correct answer is c. (CMA December 1993, 3-24)

PROCESS COSTING

Learning Objectives

After reading and studying Chapter 7, you should be able to:

1. Differentiate process costing from job order product costing.

2. Understand why equivalent units of production are used in process costing.

3. Compute equivalent units of production using the weighted average and FIFO methods of process costing.

4. Calculate unit costs and inventory values using the weighted average and FIFO methods of process costing.

5. Prepare a production and cost report.

6. Understand how standard costs are used in a process costing system.

7. Determine how multidepartment processing affects the computation of equivalent units of production.

8. Discuss how quality control can minimize spoilage.

9. (Appendix) Prepare journal entries for a process costing system.

Terminology

Equivalent units of production (EUP) An approximation of the number of whole units of output that could have been produced during a period from the actual effort expended during that period

FIFO method A method of process costing that computes an average cost per equivalent unit of production using only current period production and current cost information; units and costs in beginning inventory are accounted for separately

Method of neglect A method of treating spoiled units in the equivalent units schedule as if they did not exist

Process costing A method of accumulating and assigning costs to units of production in companies that make large quantities of homogeneous products

Process costing system A costing system in which costs are accumulated for each cost component in each department and assigned to all of the units that flow through the department

Production and cost report A document used in a process costing system; details all manufacturing quantities and costs, shows the computation of cost per EUP, and indicates the cost assignment to goods produced during the period

Statistical process control (SPC) Techniques that are used to analyze whether processes are in or out of control; based on the theory that a process varies naturally over time but that uncommon variations also occur and are typically the points at which the process produces errors, which may be defective or spoiled goods or poor service

Total cost to account for The balance in Work in Process Inventory at the beginning of the period plus all current costs for direct materials, direct labor, and factory overhead

Total units to account for All units that were worked on in the department during the current period; consists of beginning inventory units plus units started

Units started and completed The total units completed during the period minus the units in beginning inventory; alternatively, units started minus units in ending inventory

Weighted average method A method of process costing that computes an average cost per equivalent unit of production; combines beginning inventory units with current production and beginning inventory costs with current costs to compute that average

Lecture Outline

A. **Introduction to Process Costing**

1. **Process costing** is a method of accumulating and assigning costs to units of production in companies that make large quantities of homogeneous products.

2. A **process costing system** is a costing system in which costs are accumulated for each cost component in each department and assigned to all of the units that flowed through the department.

   a. Units are transferred from one department to the next; unit costs are also transferred so that a total production cost is accumulated by the end of production.

   b. The accumulated departmental costs are spread or assigned to all units produced that flowed through the department during the period.

3. The two basic differences between job order and process costing are: (1) the quantity of production for which costs are being accumulated at any one time and (2) the cost object to which the costs are assigned.

4. The three other differences between job order and process costing – a process costing system would: (1) produce homogeneous rather than heterogeneous products, (2) use continuous processing rather than specific processing, and (3) use a production and cost report rather than a job order cost sheet.

5. Cost assignment in any production environment is essentially an averaging process.

6. The average unit cost of a product is found by dividing a period's departmental production costs by the period's departmental quantity of production, the average being expressed by the following formula:

$$\text{Unit Cost per Period} = \frac{\text{Sum of Production Costs}}{\text{Quantity of Production}}$$

   a. The numerator in the average product cost fraction is the sum of the: ① actual direct materials cost, ② actual direct labor cost, and ③ actual or predetermined overhead cost.

   b. The denominator in the average product cost fraction represents total departmental production for the period.

7. **Equivalent units of production (EUP)** are an approximation of the number of whole units of output that could have been produced during a period from the actual effort expended during that period. Two facts are recognized by the use of equivalent units of production.

   a. Units in the beginning Work in Process Inventory were started last period, but will be completed during the current period – meaning that some costs related to these units were incurred last period and additional costs will be incurred in the current period.

   b. Partially completed units in the ending Work in Process Inventory were started in the current period, but will not be completed until the next period – so that current production efforts on the ending Work in Process Inventory caused costs to be incurred in this period and will cause additional costs to be incurred next period.

B. **Introducing Weighted Average and FIFO Process Costing**

   1. The **weighted average method** is a method of process costing that computes an average cost per equivalent unit of production; combines beginning inventory units with current production and beginning inventory costs with current costs to compute that average.

   a. The weighted average method is **not** concerned about what quantity of work was performed in the prior period on the units in beginning inventory; it only focuses on units that are **completed** in the current period and units remaining in ending inventory.

b. The method does **not** distinguish between units in beginning inventory and units entering production during a period.

c. Average unit cost is determined by dividing the total cost to be accounted for by the total equivalent units of production and is calculated as follows:

$$\text{Average WA Unit Cost} = \frac{\text{BWIP Cost} + \text{Current Period Cost}}{\text{Total WA EUP}}$$

2. The **FIFO method** is a method of process costing that computes an average cost per equivalent unit of production using only current period production and cost information; units and costs in beginning inventory are accounted for separately.

a. The FIFO method more realistically reflects the way in which most goods actually flow through the production system.

b. The method does **not** commingle units and costs of different periods, so that equivalent units and costs of beginning inventory are withheld from the computation of average current period cost.

c. The focus is specifically on the work performed during the current period, and the EUP schedule shows only that work.

d. The FIFO average cost per equivalent unit is calculated as follows:

$$\text{Average FIFO Unit Cost} = \frac{\text{Current Period Costs}}{\text{Total FIFO EUP}}$$

C. **EUP Calculations and Cost Assignment**

1. Six steps are necessary to determine the costs assignable to completed units and to units still in process at the end of a period in a process costing system. (see text **Exhibit 7-4**):

a. Calculate the total physical units for which the department is responsible, or the **total units to account for**.

b. Determine what happened to the units to account for during the period: units be categorized as either ① completed and transferred or ② partially completed and remaining in Work in Process Inventory.

  c. Determine the equivalent units of production for each cost component by using either the weighted average or the FIFO method.

  d. Find the **total cost to account for**, which includes the beginning balance in Work in Process Inventory plus all current costs for direct materials, direct labor, and factory overhead.

  e. Calculate the cost per equivalent unit for each cost component by using either the weighted average or the FIFO equivalents of production calculated in step c.

  f. Use the costs calculated in step e to assign the costs to the units completed and transferred from the production process and to the units in ending Work in Process Inventory.

  g. A **production and cost report** is a document used in a process costing system; details all manufacturing quantities and costs, shows the computation of cost per EUP, and indicates the cost assignment to goods produced during the period. Commonly called a **cost of production report**. (see text **Exhibit 7-6**)

D. **Process Costing with Standard Costs**

  1. Standard cost usage simplifies process costing and allows variances to be measured during the period.

  2. Standard costing eliminates the periodic recomputation of production cost that is required under actual costing.

  3. Equivalent unit calculations for standard process costing are identical to those of FIFO process costing.

E. **Process Costing in a Multidepartment Setting** (See text **Exhibits 7-6, 7-7, and 7-8**)

  1. Goods are transferred from a predecessor department to a successor department.

  2. A successor department may or may not add additional raw materials to the units that have been transferred in or may simply provide additional labor with the corresponding incurrence of overhead.

  3. Successor departments may change the unit of measure from that of predecessor departments.

F. Reducing Spoilage by Implementing Quality Processes

1. Many companies have great difficulty in determining the actual cost of spoilage.

   a. The **method of neglect** is a method of treating spoiled units in the equivalent units schedule as if they did not exist.

   b. The exclusion of spoiled units from process costing equivalent unit calculations effectively conceals from managers the magnitude of the costs of spoiled units.

   c. The inclusion of spoilage cost in the calculation of the overhead rate in job order costing also conceals spoilage cost from management.

2. Managers may be able to determine the reasons for spoilage or poor service but may not be making such a determination for the following reasons.

   a. The managers may believe that the cause creates only a minimal amount of spoilage. Such an attitude can institute spoilage tolerance levels that become rationalizations for problems.

   b. The embodiment of such tolerance levels into the production/performance system and combining the tolerance levels with the previously mentioned method of neglect will result in managers not being furnished with the necessary information they need to determine the company's spoilage cost.

3. Managers may believe that spoilage is uncontrollable.

   a. Such a belief may be correct.

   b. Companies are deciding that if quality is *built into* the process, there will be less need for inspections or surveys since spoilage and poor service will be minimized, making the goal process control rather than output *inspection and observation*.

   c. Companies that institute quality programs in order to minimize defects and/or poor service often employ **statistical process control (SPC)** which consists of techniques that are used to analyze whether processes are in or out of control, and is based on the theory that a process varies naturally over time but that uncommon variations also occur and are typically the points at which the process produces errors, which may be defective or spoiled goods or poor service. (see text **Chapter 2**.

d. The utmost managerial emphasis concerning spoilage is in *controlling* it rather than *accounting for* spoilage costs.

G. Journal Entries Related to Royalty Bakery – **Appendix**

Multiple Choice Questions from CMA Examinations

Questions 1 through 4 concern Levittown Company, which employs a process cost system for its manufacturing operations. All direct materials are added at the beginning of the process and conversion costs are added proportionately. Levittown's production quantity schedule for November is reproduced below.

	Units
Work-in-process on November 1 (60% complete as to conversion costs)	1,000
Units started during November	5,000
Total units to account for	6,000
Units completed and transferred out from beginning inventory	1,000
Units started and completed during November	3,000
Work-in-process on November 30 (20% complete as to conversion costs)	2,000
Total units accounted for	6,000

1. Using the FIFO method, the equivalent units for direct materials for November are:
   a. 5,000 units.
   b. 6,000 units.
   c. 4,400 units.
   d. 3,800 units.
   e. some amount other than those given above.

   The correct answer is a. (CMA December 1986, 4-14)

2. Using the FIFO method, the equivalent units for conversion costs for November are:

   a. 3,400 units.
   b. 3,800 units.
   c. 4,000 units.
   d. 4,400 units.
   e. some amount other than those given above.

   The correct answer is b. (CMA December 1986, 4-15)

3. Using the weighted average method, the equivalent units for direct materials for November are:
   a. 3,400 units.
   b. 4,400 units.
   c. 5,000 units.
   d. 6,000 units.
   e. some amount other than those given above.

The correct answer is d. (CMA December 1986, 4-16)

4. Using the weighted average method, the equivalent units for conversion costs for November are:

   a. 3,400 units.
   b. 3,800 units.
   c. 4,000 units.
   d. 4,400 units.
   e. some amount other than those given above.

The correct answer is d. (CMA December 1986, 4-17)

Solution

FIFO:

Materials:	Total Units				Equivalent Units
Beginning WIP inventory	1,000	X	0%	=	-0-
Started and completed	3,000	X	100%	=	3,000
Ending WIP inventory	2,000	X	100%	=	2,000
Totals	6,000				5,000

Conversion:	Total Units				Equivalent Units
Beginning WIP inventory	1,000	X	40%	=	400
Started and completed	3,000	X	100%	=	3,000
Ending WIP inventory	2,000	X	20%	=	400
Totals	6,000				3,800

Weighted Average:

Materials:

	Total Units				Equivalent Units
Beginning WIP inventory	1,000	X	100%	=	1,000
Started and completed	3,000	X	100%	=	3,000
Ending WIP inventory	2,000	X	100%	=	2,000
Totals	6,000				6,000

Conversion:

	Total Units				Equivalent Units
Beginning WIP inventory	1,000	X	100%	=	1,000
Started and completed	3,000	X	100%	=	3,000
Ending WIP inventory	2,000	X	20%	=	400
Totals	6,000				4,400

VARIABLE COSTING AND COST-VOLUME-PROFIT ANALYSIS

Learning Objectives

After reading and studying Chapter 4, you should be able to:

1. Distinguish between absorption and variable costing.

2. Determine how changes in sales and/or production levels affect net income computed under absorption and variable costing.

3. Convert variable costing information to absorption costing information.

4. Compute breakeven point and understand what it represents.

5. Recognize how costs, revenues, and contribution margin interact with changes in an activity base (volume).

6. Contrast cost-volume-profit (CVP) analysis in single-product and multiproduct firms.

7. Explain how the margin of safety and operating leverage concepts are used in business.

8. Explain the underlying assumptions of CVP analysis and how these assumptions create a short-run managerial perspective.

9. Discuss how quality decisions affect the components of CVP analysis.

10. (Appendix) Prepare breakeven and profit-volume graphs.

Terminology

Absorption costing A cost accumulation method that treats the costs of all manufacturing components (direct materials, direct labor, variable overhead, and fixed overhead) as inventoriable, or product, costs; also known as full costing

Breakeven graph A graphical depiction of the relationships among revenues, variable costs, fixed costs, and profits (or losses) (from **appendix**)

Breakeven point (BEP) The level of activity, in units or dollars, at which total revenues equal total costs

Contribution margin (CM) Selling price per unit minus all variable production, selling, and administrative costs per unit

Contribution margin ratio (CM%) Contribution margin divided by revenue; indicates what proportion of selling price remains after variable costs have been covered

Cost-volume-profit (CVP) analysis A process of examining the relationships among revenues, costs, and profits for a relevant range of activity and for a particular time frame

Degree of operating leverage (DOL) A measure of how a percentage change in sales will affect profits

Functional classification A grouping of costs incurred for the same basic purpose

Incremental analysis A process that focuses only on factors that change from one course of action or decision to another

Margin of safety The excess of the budgeted or actual sales of a company over its breakeven point

Operating leverage A factor that reflects the relationship of a company's variable and fixed costs; measures the change in profits expected to result from a specified change in sales

Product contribution margin Revenue minus variable cost of goods sold

Profit-volume (PV) graph A graphical presentation of the profit or loss associated with each level of sales (from **appendix**)

Total contribution margin Revenue minus all variable costs regardless of the area (production or nonproduction) of incurrence

Variable costing A cost accumulation method that includes only variable production costs (direct materials, direct labor, and variable overhead) as product or inventoriable costs and treats fixed overhead as a period cost; also known as direct costing

Lecture Outline

A. An Overview of Absorption and Variable Costing

1. **Absorption costing** is a cost accumulation method that treats the costs of all manufacturing components (direct materials, direct labor, variable overhead, and fixed overhead) as inventoriable or product costs; also known as full costing. (see text **Exhibit 8-1**)

   a. Absorption costing presents expenses on an income statement according to their functional classifications. A **functional classification** is a grouping of costs that were all incurred for the same basic purpose.

   b. Total variable product costs increase with each additional product made or service rendered, and are therefore considered to be product costs and are inventoried until the product or service is sold.

   c. Fixed overhead does not vary with units of production or level of service; it provides the manufacturing capacity necessary for production to occur. Production could not take place without the incurrence of fixed overhead, so fixed overhead is considered to be inventoriable under absorption costing.

   d. Absorption costing is perceived to furnish external parties with a more informative picture of earnings, as compared to variable costing, by authoritative accounting bodies such as the FASB and the SEC.

   e. The IRS requires absorption costing for income tax purposes.

2. **Variable costing** is a cost accumulation method that includes only variable production costs (direct materials, direct labor, and variable overhead) as product or inventoriable costs and treats fixed overhead as a period cost; it is also known as direct costing. (see text **Exhibit 8-2**)

   a. A variable costing income statement presents expenses according to cost behavior (variable and fixed), although it may present expenses by functional classification within the behavioral categories.

   b. Cost of goods sold is more appropriately called *variable* cost of goods sold since it is composed of only the variable production costs related to the units sold.

c. **Product contribution margin** is revenue minus variable cost of goods sold, and indicates how much revenue is available to cover all period expenses and to potentially provide net income. Product contribution margin is also called manufacturing margin.

d. **Total contribution margin** is revenue minus all variable costs regardless of the area (production or nonproduction) of incurrence.

e. The accounting profession has unofficially disallowed the use of variable costing as a generally accepted inventory valuation method for external reporting purposes.

B. **Absorption and Variable Costing Illustrations** (see text **Exhibits 8-3, 8-4, 8-5 and 8-6**)

1. The two basic differences between absorption and variable costing are:

   a. Fixed overhead is considered to be a product cost under absorption costing, while it is treated as a period cost under variable costing.

   b. Absorption costing classifies costs by function, while variable costing categorizes costs by behavior and, then potentially, by function.

2. The two costing methods have four underlying similarities: (1) both methods use the same basic cost information; (2) direct materials, direct labor, and variable overhead are all treated as product costs under each method; (3) selling, general, and administrative expenses are considered to be period costs under both methods; and (4) differences between accounts are found only in Work in Process Inventory, Finished Goods Inventory, and the expense accounts under the two methods.

3. Absorption costing income will equal variable costing income if production is equal to sales.

4. Absorption costing income will be greater than variable costing income if production is greater than sales.

   a. Some fixed overhead cost is deferred as part of inventory cost on the balance sheet under absorption costing.

   b. The total amount of fixed overhead cost is expensed as a period cost under variable costing.

5. Absorption costing income will be less than variable costing income if production is less than sales.

   a. Absorption costing expenses all of the current period fixed overhead cost as well as releasing some fixed overhead cost from inventory.

   b. Variable costing shows on the income statement only current period fixed overhead, so that the additional amount released from beginning inventory makes absorption costing income lower.

   c. Income manipulation is made possible by the process of deferring and releasing fixed overhead costs in and from inventory under absorption costing, leading some to believe that variable costing might be more useful for external reporting purposes than absorption costing.

6. The four categories of differences between absorption and variable costing (see text **Exhibit 8-7**) are: (1) composition of product cost, (2) structure of the chart of accounts, (3) process of accumulating costs, and (4) format of the income statement.

7. A company would need to make working paper entries at year-end to increase its inventory and cost of goods sold accounts for the fixed overhead cost per unit for the purpose of restating reports from variable to absorption costing.

   a. A volume variance would need to be recorded if the actual fixed overhead allocation base differed from the estimated base.

   b. A single amount would be shown on the absorption costing income statement for the sum of the separate variable and fixed accounts for each of the functional classifications.

C. The Breakeven Point

1. The **breakeven point (BEP)** is the level of activity, in units or dollars, at which total revenues equal total costs.

2. Basic simplifying assumptions about revenue and cost functions:

 a. *Revenue*: Total revenue fluctuates in direct proportion to units sold, while revenue per unit is assumed to remain constant; fluctuations in per unit revenue for factors such as quantity discounts are ignored.

 b. *Variable costs*: Total variable costs fluctuate in direct proportion to level of activity or volume. Variable costs per unit remain constant within the *relevant range*. Variable costs exist in all functional business areas including production, distribution, selling, and administrative.

 c. *Fixed costs*: Total fixed costs remain constant within the *relevant range*. Fixed cost per unit decreases as volume increases, and it increases as volume decreases. Fixed costs include **both** fixed factory overhead and fixed selling and administrative expenses.

 d. *Mixed costs*: Mixed costs must be separated into their variable and fixed elements before they can be used in breakeven analysis. Any method that validly separates these costs in relation to one or more predictors may be used.

2. **Contribution margin (CM)** is defined as selling price per unit minus all variable production, selling, and administrative costs per unit.

3. **Total contribution margin** is revenue minus all variable costs regardless of the area (production or nonproduction) of incurrence; it fluctuates in direct proportion to sales volume.

4. The formula approach to breakeven uses an algebraic equation to calculate the breakeven point.

 a. The answer to the equation is not always an "acceptable" solution, since partial units cannot be sold or some items may only be sold in specified lot sizes.

 b. The answers provided by solving the equations may need to be rounded to whole numbers, and the rounding is always done upwards in breakeven analysis; a small profit rather than a small loss will be provided by such rounding.

 c. The **contribution margin ratio (CM%)** is the contribution margin divided by revenue; indicates what proportion of selling price remains after variable costs have been covered.

d. Algebraic breakeven computations use an equation that represents the income statement and groups costs by behavior to show the relationships among revenue, fixed cost, variable cost, volume, and profit as follows:

$$R(X) - VC(X) - FC = P$$

R = revenue (selling price) per unit
X = number of units sold or to be sold
$R(X)$ = total revenue
FC = total fixed cost
VC = variable cost per unit
$VC(X)$ = total variable cost
P = before-tax profit

e. Total revenues are equal to total costs plus profit; this relationship is shown by slightly reformatting the equation:

$$R(X) = VC(X) + FC + P$$

f. The equation represents an income statement, so P can be set equal to zero for the formula to indicate a breakeven situation. The breakeven point in units to be sold can be found by solving the equation for X:

$$X = FC \div (R - VC)$$

g. Breakeven volume is equal to total fixed cost divided by (revenue per unit minus variable cost per unit); the formula can be abbreviated as follows using contribution margin to find the breakeven point:

$$X = FC \div CM$$

where CM = contribution margin per unit

h. The BEP can be expressed in either units or dollars of revenue – ① the BEP in sales dollars can be found by multiplying the BEP in units by the selling price per unit or ② the BEP in sales dollars can also be found by dividing total fixed cost by the CM%.

i. The BEP provides a starting point for planning future operations.

D. **CVP Analysis** (see text **Exhibits 8-11, 8-12, and 8-13**)

1. **Cost-volume-profit (CVP) analysis** is a process of examining the relationships among revenues, costs, and profits for a relevant range of activity and for a particular time frame. The technique is applicable in all economic sectors (manufacturing, wholesaling, retailing, and service industries) since the same types of managerial functions are performed in each type of organization.

2. CVP analysis uses the same algebraic income statement formula that is used for the calculation of the breakeven point, but includes a profit amount.

3. A significant application of CVP analysis is the setting of a desired target profit and focusing on the relationships between it and specified income statement amounts to find an unknown.

   a. Volume is a common unknown in such applications since managers want to achieve a particular amount of profit and need to know what quantity of sales needs to be generated to accomplish this objective.

   b. Selling price is not as common an unknown as volume since selling price is usually market-related rather than being set solely by company management.

4. Profits may be stated either as a fixed or variable amount and on either a before-tax or after-tax basis.

5. The amount of profit may be specified — after the breakeven point is reached, each dollar of contribution margin is a dollar of profit.

   a. The formula would appear as follows for a fixed amount of profit before taxes:

$$X = (FC + PBT) \div (R - VC) \qquad \text{where } X = \text{units}$$
$$\text{or}$$
$$X = (FC + PBT) \div CM \qquad \text{where } X = \text{units}$$
$$\text{or}$$
$$X = (FC + PBT) \div CM\% \qquad \text{where } X = \text{dollars}$$

   where   PBT = specified amount of profit before taxes
   CM% = contribution margin ratio

b. The formula would appear as follows for a fixed amount of profit after taxes:

$$R(X) = VC(X) + FC + PBT$$
$$\text{and}$$
$$PBT = PAT \div (1 - TR)$$
$$\text{so}$$
$$X = (FC + PBT) \div CM$$

where   PAT = specified amount of profit after taxes and TR = tax rate

6. Managers may want desired profit to be equal to a specified variable amount of sales.

a. The formula would appear as follows for a variable amount of profit before taxes:

$$R(X) = VC(X) + FC + P_u BT(X)$$
$$\text{or}$$
$$X = FC \div (CM - P_u BT)$$

where $P_u BT$ = desired profit per unit before taxes

b. The formula would appear as follows for a variable amount of profit after taxes:

$$R(X) = VC(X) + FC + P_u BT(X)$$
$$\text{and}$$
$$P_u BT(X) = [P_u AT \div (1 - TR)] (X)$$
$$\text{so}$$
$$X = FC \div (CM - P_u BT)$$

where $P_u AT$ = desired profit per unit after taxes

E. **Incremental Analysis for Short-Run Changes** (see text **Exhibit 8-14**)

1. The breakeven point may increase or decrease, depending on the particular changes that occur in the revenue and cost factors.

a. The breakeven point will increase if there is an increase in total fixed cost, a decrease in selling price, or an increase in variable costs.

b. A decrease in unit contribution margin is caused by a decrease in selling price, an increase in variable costs, or a combination of the two.

      c. The breakeven point will decrease if there is a decrease in total fixed cost or an increase in unit or percentage contribution margin.

      d. Any factor that causes a change in the breakeven point will also cause a shift in total profits or losses at any level of activity.

  2. **Incremental analysis** is a process that focuses only on factors that change from one course of action or decision to another. Incremental analysis is based on changes occurring in revenues, costs, and/or volume.

F. **CVP Analysis in a Multiproduct Environment** (see text **Exhibit 8-15**)

  1. A constant product sales mix or, alternatively, an average contribution margin ratio must be assumed in order to perform CVP analysis in a multiproduct company.

      a. The constant sales mix assumption can be referred to as the "bag" (or "basket") assumption, with sales mix representing a bag of products that are sold together.

      b. The computation of a weighted average contribution margin ratio for the bag of products being sold is necessary under the constant sales mix assumption.

  2. Any shift in the sales mix proportion of products will change the weighted average contribution margin and the breakeven point.

G. **Underlying Assumptions of CVP Analysis**

  1. The cost-volume-profit model is a useful planning tool that can provide information on the impact on profits when changes are made in the costing system or in sales levels.

      a. The cost-volume-profit model reflects, but does not duplicate, reality.

      b. Cost-volume-profit is a tool that focuses on the short-run partially because of the assumptions that underlie the computations.

      c. The assumptions are necessary, but they limit the accuracy of the results.

2. The underlying assumptions of CVP analysis are:

   a. All variable cost and revenue behavior patterns are constant per unit and linear within the relevant range.

   b. Total contribution margin is linear within the relevant range and increases proportionally with output.

   c. Total fixed cost is a constant amount within the relevant range.

   d. Mixed costs can be accurately separated into their fixed and variable elements. Accuracy of this separation is particularly unrealistic, but reliable estimates can be developed from the high-low method or least squares regression analysis.

   e. Sales and production are equal; thus, there is no material fluctuation in inventory levels. This assumption is necessary because of the allocation of fixed costs to inventory at potentially different rates each year.

   f. No capacity additions will be made during the period under consideration. Any such additions would change fixed (and possibly variable) costs, invalidating the first three assumptions.

   g. Sales mix will remain constant in a multiproduct firm. No useful weighted average contribution margin could be computed for CVP analysis without this assumption.

   h. Inflation does not exist or, if it can be forecasted, it is incorporated into the CVP model.

   i. Labor productivity, production technology, and market conditions will not change. Any such changes would change costs correspondingly, and possibly selling prices would change, invalidating the first three assumptions.

3. A long-term variable cost is a cost that was traditionally viewed as a fixed cost. (see text **Chapter 4**)

H. **Costs and Quality**

1. A total quality management (TQM) program is a long-run change that may create substantial short-run costs. A TQM program usually causes an increase in prevention costs which may not be offset in the short run by the decreases in appraisal and failure costs.

2. Cost, price, and volume work hand-in-hand with a fourth factor – quality.

3. The quality specifications of a product and its components will play an important part in influencing costs, and quality products are typically able to command higher selling prices.

4. The CVP component elements must be reevaluated frequently enough to compensate for changes that have occurred if such CVP elements are sensitive to continuous quality improvement efforts.

I. **Margin of Safety and Operating Leverage**

1. The **margin of safety** is the excess of the budgeted or actual sales of a company over its breakeven point; can be calculated in units or dollars or as a percentage; is equal to $1 \div$ degree of operating leverage. (see text **Exhibit 8-16**)

2. The margin of safety is the amount that sales can drop before reaching the breakeven point and, thus, provides a certain amount of "cushion" from losses.

3. The following formulae are applicable for the margin of safety:

a. Margin of safety in units = Actual units - Breakeven units

b. Margin of safety in dollars = Actual sales dollars - Breakeven sales dollars

c. Margin of safety % = $\dfrac{\text{Margin of safety in units}}{\text{Actual sales in units}}$

d. Margin of safety % = $\dfrac{\text{Margin of safety in dollars}}{\text{Actual sales in dollars}}$

4. The margin of safety calculation allows management to determine how close to a danger level the company is operating, and thus provides an indication of risk.

5. **Operating leverage** is a factor that reflects the relationship of a company's variable and fixed costs; measures the change in profits expected to result from a specified change in sales.

6. Low operating leverage and a relatively low breakeven point are found in companies that are highly labor-intensive, have high variable costs, and low fixed costs.

   a. Companies with low operating leverage can experience wide swings in volume levels and still show a profit.

   b. An exception is a sports team, which is highly labor-intensive, but whose labor costs are fixed.

7. High operating leverage and a relatively high breakeven point are found in companies that have low variable costs and high fixed costs.

   a. Companies will face this type of cost structure and become more dependent on volume to add profits as they become more automated.

   b. Companies with high operating leverage also have high contribution margin ratios.

8. The **degree of operating leverage** is a measure of how a percentage change in sales will affect profits; calculated as contribution margin divided by profit before taxes; is equal to 1 ÷ margin of safety percentage. The computation providing the degree of operating leverage factor is:

$$\text{Degree of operating leverage} = \frac{\text{Contribution margin}}{\text{Profit before taxes}}$$

   a. The calculation assumes that fixed costs do not increase when sales increase.

   b. The degree of operating leverage decreases the further a company moves from its breakeven point; when the margin of safety is small, the degree of operating leverage is large.

J. Graphic Approaches to Breakeven Analysis – Appendix

1. A **breakeven graph** is a graphical depiction of the relationships among revenues, variable costs, fixed costs, and profits (or losses).

2. The **traditional approach** to graphical breakeven analysis is a breakeven graph that does *not* show contribution margin.

3. The **contemporary approach** specifically presents CM in the breakeven graph. The contemporary approach allows the following important observations to be made:

   a. Contribution margin is created by the excess of revenues over **variable** costs; if variable costs are greater than revenues, no quantity of volume will ever allow a profit to be made.

   b. Total contribution margin is *always* equal to total fixed cost plus profit or minus loss.

   c. Contribution margin must exceed fixed costs before profits can be generated.

4. The **profit-volume (PV) graph** is a graphical representation of the amount of profit or loss associated with each level of sales. (see text **Exhibit 8-20**)

   a. The horizontal axis on the PV graph represents unit sales volume and the vertical axis represents dollars.

   b. Amounts shown above the horizontal axis are positive and represent profits, while amounts below the horizontal axis are negative and represent losses.

Multiple Choice Questions from CMA Examinations

1. Which of the following statements is true for a firm that uses direct (variable) costing?
   a. The cost of a unit of product changes because of changes in the number of units manufactured.
   b. Profits fluctuate with sales.
   c. An idle facility variation is calculated.
   d. Product costs include "direct" (variable) administrative costs.
   e. None of the above.

   The correct answer is b. (CMA December 1973, 4-1)

2. When a firm prepares financial reports by using absorption costing,
   a. profits will always increase with increases in sales.
   b. profits will always decrease with decreases in sales.
   c. profits may decrease with increased sales even if there is no change in selling prices and costs.
   d. decreased output and constant sales result in increased profits.
   e. none of the above.

   The correct answer is c. (CMA December 1973, 4-2)

Questions 3 and 4 are based on the following information. Valyn Corporation employs an absorption costing system for internal reporting purposes; however, the company is considering using variable costing. Data regarding Valyn's planned and actual operations for the 1994 calendar year are presented below.

	Planned Activity	Actual Activity
Beginning finished goods inventory in units	35,000	35,000
Sales in units	140,000	125,000
Production in units	140,000	130,000

The planned per unit cost figures shown in the next schedule were based on the estimated production and sale of 140,000 units in 1994. Valyn uses a predetermined manufacturing overhead rate for applying manufacturing overhead to its product; thus, a combined manufacturing overhead rate of $9.00 per unit was employed for absorption costing purposes in 1994. Any over- or underapplied manufacturing overhead is closed to the cost of goods sold account at the end of the reporting year.

	Planned Costs		Incurred
	Per Unit	Total	Costs
Direct material	$12.00	$1,680,000	$1,560,000
Direct labor	9.00	1,260,000	1,170,000
Variable manufacturing overhead	4.00	560,000	520,000
Fixed manufacturing overhead	5.00	700,000	715,000
Variable selling expenses	8.00	1,120,000	1,000,000
Fixed selling expenses	7.00	980,000	980,000
Variable administrative expenses	2.00	280,000	250,000
Fixed administrative expenses	3.00	420,000	425,000
Totals	$50.00	$7,000,000	$6,620,000

The 1994 beginning finished goods inventory for absorption costing purposes was valued at the 1993 planned unit manufacturing cost, which was the same as the 1994 planned unit manufacturing cost. There are no work-in-process inventories at either the beginning or the end of the year. The planned and actual unit selling price for 1994 was $70.00 per unit.

3. Valyn Corporation's absorption costing operating income in 1994 was:
   a. higher than variable costing operating income because actual production exceeded actual sales.
   b. lower than variable costing operating income because actual production exceeded actual sales.
   c. lower than variable costing operating income because actual production was less than planned production.
   d. lower than variable costing operating income because actual sales were less than planned sales.
   e. higher than variable costing operating income because planned production exceeded actual sales.

The correct answer is a. (CMA December 1990, 3-29)

4. The difference between Valyn Corporation's 1994 operating income calculated on the absorption costing basis and calculated on the variable costing basis was:

a. $ 65,000.
b. $ 25,000.
c. $ 40,000.
d. $ 90,000.
e. $200,000.

The correct answer is b. (CMA December 1990, 3-30)

Solutions

VALYN CORPORATION
Income Statement
For the Year Ended December 31, 1994

Sales		$ 8,750,000
Cost of Sales:		
Finished goods – January 1, 1994	$ 1,050,000	
Cost of goods manufactured	3,900,000	
Goods available for sale	4,950,000	
Finished goods – December 31, 1994	<1,200,000>	
Cost of sales – unadjusted	3,750,000	
Overhead variance	65,000	<3,815,000>
Gross margin		4,935,000
Operating expenses:		
Selling expenses		
Administrative expenses		<2,655,000>
Operating income		$ 2,280,000

VALYN CORPORATION
Contribution Income Statement
For the Year Ended December 31, 1994

Sales		$ 8,750,000
Variable cost of Sales:		
Finished goods – January 1, 1994	$ 875,000	
Cost of goods manufactured	3,250,000	
Goods available for sale	4,125,000	
Finished goods – December 31, 1994	<1,000,000>	<3,125,000>
Manufacturing margin		5,625,000
Variable operating expenses		<1,250,000>
Contribution margin		4,375,000
Fixed costs and expenses:		
Fixed overhead	715,000	
Fixed selling expenses	980,000	
Fixed administrative expenses	425,000	<2,120,000>
Operating income		$ 2,255,000

The following data apply to questions 5-7.

Delphi Company has developed a new product that will be marketed for the first time during the next fiscal year. Although the Marketing Department estimates that 35,000 units could be sold at $36 per unit, Delphi's management has allocated only enough manufacturing capacity to produce a maximum of 25,000 units of the new product annually. The fixed costs associated with the new product are budgeted at $450,000 for the year which includes $60,000 for depreciation on new manufacturing equipment. Data associated with each unit of product are presented below. Delphi is subject to a 40% income tax rate.

	Variable Costs
Direct material	$ 7.00
Direct labor	3.50
Manufacturing overhead	4.00
Total variable manufacturing cost	$ 14.50
Selling expenses	1.50
Total variable cost	$ 16.00

5. The number of units of the new product that Delphi Company must sell during the next fiscal year in order to break even is:
   a. 20,930.
   b. 18,140.
   c. 22,500.
   d. 19,500.
   e. 25,500.

   The correct answer is c. (CMA June 1993, 4-1)

6. The maximum after-tax profit that can be earned by Delphi Company from sales of the new product during the next fiscal year is:
   a. $ 30,000.
   b. $ 50,000.
   c. $110,000.
   d. $ 66,000.
   e. $150,000.

   The correct answer is a. (CMA June 1993, 4-2)

7. Delphi Company's management has stipulated that it will not approve the continued manufacture of the new product after the next fiscal year unless the after-tax profit is at least $75,000 the first year. The unit selling price to achieve this target profit must be at least:
   a. $37.00
   b. $36.60.
   c. $34.60.
   d. $41.40.
   e. $39.00.

   The correct answer is e. (CMA June 1993, 4-3)

Solutions

	Per Unit	5. Breakeven 22,500 *	6. 25,000
Sales	$36.00	$ 810,000	$ 900,000
Variable costs	<16.00>	<360,000>	<400,000>
Contribution margin	$20.00	450,000	500,000
Fixed costs		<450,000>	<450,000>
Pretax income		$ -0-	50,000
Income tax expense			<20,000>
Net income <loss>			$ 30,000
			6.

* $450,000 ÷ $20 = 22,500 units.

7.

	Per Unit	25,000
Sales	$39.00 *	$ 975,000
Variable costs	<16.00>	<400,000>
Contribution margin	$23.00	575,000
Fixed costs		<450,000>
Pretax income		125,000
Income tax expense		<50,000>
Net income <loss>		$ 75,000

* $575,000 ÷ 25,000 units = $23 + $16 = $39.

RELEVANT COSTING

Learning Objectives

After reading and studying Chapter 9, you should be able to:

1. Determine what constitutes relevance in a decision-making situation.

2. Understand why a sunk cost (such as joint cost) is not relevant in decision making, but an opportunity cost is.

3. Recognize the quantitative and qualitative factors that need to be considered in making decisions with multiple alternative outcomes.

4. Specify the relevant costs that exist in a make-or-buy situation.

5. Determine how management can best utilize a scarce resource.

6. Relate sales mix to relevant costing problems.

7. Make pricing decisions to maximize profit.

8. Use product margin to determine whether a product line should be retained or eliminated.

9. (Appendix) Describe the elements of a linear programming problem.

Terminology

Constraint A restriction on the ability to reach an objective (from **appendix**)

Feasible solution An answer to a linear programming problem that does not violate any of the problem constraints (from **appendix**)

Incremental cost The additional cost of producing or selling a contemplated quantity of output

Incremental revenue The additional revenue resulting from a contemplated sale of a quantity of output

Joint cost The cost incurred, up to the split-off point, for materials, labor, and overhead in a joint process

Joint process A process in which one product cannot be manufactured without others being produced

Linear programming A method used to solve problems with one objective and multiple limiting factors; finds the optimal allocation of scarce resources when the objective and the restrictions on achieving that objective can be stated as linear equations

Make-or-buy decision A decision that compares the cost of internally manufacturing a product component with the cost of purchasing it from outside suppliers or from another division at a specified transfer price and, thus, attempts to assess the best use of available facilities

Objective function The mathematical equation that states the maximization or minimization goal of a linear programming problem (from **appendix**)

Optimal solution The solution to a linear programming problem that provides the best answer to the allocation problem without violating any problem constraints (from **appendix**)

Opportunity cost The benefit foregone when one course of action is chosen over another

Outsource To buy a service or component from an external provider

Product margin The excess of a product's revenues over both its direct variable expenses and any avoidable fixed expenses related to the product; the amount remaining to cover unavoidable direct fixed expenses and common costs and then to provide profits

Relevant cost A cost that is pertinent to or logically associated with a specific problem or decision and that differs between alternatives

Relevant costing A process that allows managers to focus on pertinent facts and disregard extraneous information by comparing, to the extent possible and practical, the differential, incremental revenues and incremental costs of alternative decisions

Sales mix The relative combination of quantities of sales of the various products that make up the total sales of a company

Scarce resource An item that is essential to production activity but that is available only in a limited quantity

Simplex An iterative technique used to solve multivariable, multiconstraint linear programming problems; usually requires the aid of a computer (from **appendix**)

Special order pricing The process of setting a sales price for manufacturing or service jobs that are outside the company's normal production or service realm

Split-off point The point at which the outputs of a joint process are first identifiable as individual products

Sunk cost The historical or past cost that is associated with the acquisition of an asset or a resource; it has no future recovery value

Lecture Outline

A. **The Concepts of Relevance and Relevant Costing**

1. **Relevant cost** is a cost that is pertinent to or logically associated with a specific problem or decision and that differs between alternatives.

2. **Relevant costing** is a process that allows managers to focus on pertinent facts and disregard extraneous information by comparing, to the extent possible and practical, the differential, incremental revenues and incremental costs of alternative decisions.

3. Relevant information supports decision making, and information is relevant when it is logically related to the decision.

4. **Incremental revenue** is the additional revenue resulting from a contemplated sale of a quantity of output.

5. **Incremental cost** is the additional cost of producing or selling a contemplated quantity of output.

   a. Incremental costs can be either variable or fixed.

   b. Most variable costs are relevant while most fixed costs are not relevant.

6. The difference between the incremental revenue and incremental costs of a particular alternative is the positive or negative incremental benefit of that course of action.

   a. Management can compare the incremental benefits of various alternatives to decide on the most profitable or least costly alternative or set of alternatives.

   b. Some relevant factors, such as sales commissions and prime product costs, are easily identified and quantified, and are integral parts of the accounting system.

   c. Other factors, such as opportunity costs, may be relevant and quantifiable, but are not part of the accounting system. An **opportunity cost** is the benefit foregone when one course of action is chosen over another.

7. The need for specific information depends on how important the information is relative to management objectives.

8. Information can be based on past or present data, but it can only be relevant if it pertains to and will be differential in relation to a future choice.

   a. The future may be the short-run or the long-run; future costs are the only costs that can be avoided; and, the longer into the future a decision's time horizon, the more costs are controllable, avoidable, and relevant.

   b. The only information that is relevant in decision-making is information that has a bearing on future events.

B. Sunk Costs and Joint Processes

1. **Sunk costs** are the historical or past costs that are associated with the acquisition of assets or resources and that have no future recovery value.

2. A **joint process** is a process in which one product cannot be manufactured without producing others.

3. **Joint products** are the primary outputs of a joint process, each of which has substantial revenue-generating ability.

4. A **by-product** is an incidental output of a joint process, and has a higher sales value than scrap.

5. **Scrap** is an incidental output of a joint process, and has a lower sales value than a by-product.

6. **Waste** is a residual output of a joint process that has no sales value.

7. The **split-off point** is the point at which the outputs of a joint process are first identifiable as individual products.

8. A **joint cost** is the cost incurred, up to the split-off point, for materials, labor, and overhead in a joint process.

   a. Costs incurred after split-off are assigned to the separate products for which those costs are incurred.

   b. The joint cost is allocated, at the split-off point, to the primary output of the production process.

C. **Relevant Costs in Make-or-Buy Decisions** (see text **Exhibits 9-2 and 9-3**)

1. A **make-or-buy decision** is a decision that compares the cost of internally manufacturing a product component with the cost of purchasing it from outside suppliers or from another division at a specified transfer price and, thus, attempts to assess the best use of available facilities.

2. Managers in manufacturing environments are constantly concerned about whether the right quality components will be available at the right time and a reasonable price to assure production, and companies often assure the availability of a component by manufacturing it themselves.

3. A typical make-or-buy decision should be made only after proper analysis, which should include comparing the cost of internally producing a component to the cost of purchasing it from outside suppliers or from other divisions at specified transfer prices, and then assessing the best use of the available facilities.

4. Variable production costs are relevant, and fixed production costs may be relevant if they can be avoided when production is discontinued.

5. The opportunity cost of the facilities being used by production may also be relevant.

6. Many service organizations also need to make the same kinds of decisions.

D. **Relevant Costs in Scarce Resource Decisions**

1. A **scarce resource** is an item that is essential to production activity but that is available only in a limited quantity.

2. Scarce resources create constraints on producing goods or providing services and can include money, machine hours, skilled labor hours, raw materials, and production capacity.

3. Management may desire and be able to obtain a greater abundance of a scarce resource in the long-run, but management must make the best current use of the scarce resources it has in the short-run.

4. The determination of the best use of a scarce resource requires that specific company objectives be recognized.

5. The outcome of a scarce resource decision will always indicate that a single type of product should be manufactured and sold when one limiting factor is involved.

6. One method of solving problems that have several limiting factors is linear programming which finds the optimal allocation of scarce resources when there is one objective and multiple restrictions on achieving that objective.

7. Company management must consider qualitative aspects of the problem in addition to the quantitative ones.

E. **Relevant Costs in Sales Mix and Sales Price Decisions**

1. **Sales mix** is the relative combination of quantities of sales of the various products that make up the total sales of a company.

2. Some important factors that affect the appropriate sales mix of a company are (1) product selling prices, (2) sales force compensation, and (3) advertising expenditures; and a change in one or all of the factors may cause a company's sales mix to shift.

3. Managers must constantly monitor the relative selling prices of company products, both in respect to each other as well as to competitors' prices.

4. Total contribution margin must be maximized in order to maximize profit.

5. **Product contribution margin (PCM)** is selling price minus total variable production costs. (see text **Chapter 8**)

   a. PCM does not consider variable selling costs.

   b. PCM can motivate a company's sales force when used as a basis for determining sales commission compensation.

6. A factor that may cause shifts in sales mix involves either adjusting the proportion of the advertising budgets respective to each product the company sells or increasing the total company advertising budget.

7. **Special order pricing** is the process of setting a sales price for manufacturing or service jobs that are outside the company's normal production or service realm.

F. Relevant Costs in Product Line Decisions

1. Operating results of multiproduct environments are frequently presented in a format that indicates separate product lines in order to make better performance evaluations.

2. Managers, in reviewing such statements, must distinguish relevant from irrelevant information in a manner that relates to the individual product lines.

3. The **product margin** is the excess of a product's revenues over both its direct variable expenses and any avoidable fixed expenses related to the product; the amount remaining to cover unavoidable direct fixed expenses and common costs and then to provide profits.

   a. The product margin is the appropriate figure on which to base continuation or elimination decisions since it measures the segment's contribution to the coverage of indirect and unavoidable costs.

   b. The product margin is also called the segment margin.

G. Linear Programming – Appendix

1. **Linear programming** is a method used to solve problems with one objective and multiple limiting factors; finds the optimal allocation of scarce resources when the objective and the restrictions on achieving that objective can be stated as linear equations.

2. The **objective function** is the mathematical equation that states the maximization or minimization goal of a linear programming problem.

3. A **constraint** is a restriction on the ability to reach an objective.

4. A **feasible solution** is an answer to a linear programming problem that does not violate any of the problem constraints.

5. The **optimal solution** is the solution to a linear programming problem that provides the best answer to the allocation problem without violating any problem constraints.

6. The **simplex** method is an iterative technique used to solve multi-variable, multiconstraint linear programming problems; usually requires the aid of a computer.

Multiple Choice Questions from CMA Examinations

1. Cohasset Company currently manufactures all components parts used in the manufacture of various hand tools. A steel handle is used in three different tools. The 1995 budget for 20,000 handles has the following unit cost:

Direct material	$ .60
Direct labor	.40
Variable overhead	.10
Fixed overhead	.20
Total unit cost	$ 1.30

R&M Steel has offered to supply 20,000 handles to Cohasset for $1.25 each, delivered. If Cohasset currently has idle capacity that cannot be used, accepting the offer will:

a. decrease the handle unit cost by $.05.
b. increase the handle unit cost by $.15.
c. decrease the handle unit cost by $.15.
d. decrease the handle unit cost by $.25.
e. increase the handle unit cost by $.05.

The correct answer is b. (CMA June 1987, 5-20)

Solution

	Unit	
Differential costs:	Make	Buy
Purchasing		$ 1.25
Direct material	$ .60	
Direct labor	.40	
Variable overhead	.10	
Total	$ 1.10	$ 1.25

2. The relevance of a particular cost to a decision is determined by the:
   a. size of the cost.
   b. riskiness of the decision.
   c. potential effect on the decision.
   d. accuracy and verifiability of the cost.
   e. number of decision variables.

The correct answer is c. (CMA December 1990, 4-11)

3. Opportunity costs are:
   a. not used for decision making.
   b. the same as variable costs.
   c. equal to historical costs.
   d. fixed costs.
   e. relevant to decision making.

The correct answer is e. (CMA December 1990, 4-12)

4. Total unit costs are:
   a. relevant for cost-volume-profit analysis.
   b. needed for determining sunk costs.
   c. irrelevant in marginal analysis.
   d. independent of the cost system used to generate them.
   e. needed for determining product contribution.

The correct answer is c. (CMA June 1991, 4-7)

5. A company's approach to a make-or-buy decision:
   a. depends on whether the company is operating at or below breakeven.
   b. depends on whether the company is operating at or below normal volume.
   c. involves an analysis of avoidable costs.
   d. should use absorption costing.
   e. should use activity-based costing.

The correct answer is c. (CMA June 1991, 4-9)

6. Sunk costs:
   a. are substitutes for opportunity costs.
   b. in and of themselves are not relevant to decision making.
   c. are relevant to decision making.
   d. are relevant to long-run decisions but not to short-run decisions.
   e. are fixed costs.

The correct answer is b. (CMA June 1991, 4-10)

7. The term relevant cost applies to all the following decision situations except the:
   a. acceptance of a special order.
   b. manufacture or purchase of component parts.
   c. determination of a product price.
   d. replacement of equipment.
   e. addition or deletion of a product line.

The correct answer is c. (CMA June 1991, 4-12)

Questions 8 and 9 are based on the following information. Management accountants are frequently asked to analyze various decision situations including the following.

1. Alternative uses of plant space, to be considered in a make/buy decision.
2. Joint production costs incurred, to be considered in a sell-at-split-off versus a process-further decision.
3. Research and development costs incurred in prior months, to be considered in a product-introduction decision.
4. The cost of a special device that is necessary if a special order is accepted.
5. The cost of obsolete inventory acquired several years ago, to be considered in a keep-versus-disposal decision.

8. The costs described in situations 1 and 4 are:
   a. prime costs.
   b. sunk costs.
   c. discretionary costs.
   d. relevant costs.
   e. differential costs.

The correct answer is d. (CMA December 1988, 5-12)

9. The costs described in situations 2, 3, and 5 are:
   a. prime costs.
   b. sunk costs.
   c. discretionary costs.
   d. relevant costs.
   e. differential costs.

The correct answer is b. (CMA December 1988, 5-13)

MANAGERIAL ASPECTS OF BUDGETING

Learning Objectives

After reading and studying Chapter 10, you should be able to:

1. Understand the importance of the budgeting process.

2. Differentiate between strategic and tactical planning.

3. Relate strategic and tactical planning to the budgeting process.

4. Understand the influence of the product life cycle stages on sales and costs.

5. Compare the benefits and disadvantages of imposed budgets and participatory budgets.

6. Explain how a budget manual facilitates the budgeting process.

7. Explain why actual revenue from a product differs from budgeted revenue.

8. Understand how the managerial function of control is related to budgeting.

9. Recognize why managers should use achievable budget targets.

Terminology

Appropriation A maximum allowable expenditure for a budget item (from **appendix**)

Budget The quantitative expression of an organization's commitment to planned activities and resource acquisition and use

Budget manual A detailed set of documents that provides information and guidelines about the budgetary process

Budget slack The intentional underestimation of revenues and/or overestimation of expenses, and may be introduced by managers

Budgeting The process of determining a financial plan for future operations

Continuous (or rolling) budget An ongoing twelve-month budget that is created by the addition of a new budget month (twelve months into the future) as each current month expires

Games A series of organized behavior patterns conforming to a set of rules that promote a defined outcome

Imposed budget A budget that is prepared by top management with little or no input from operating personnel, who are simply informed of the budget goals and constraints

Key variable A critical factor believed to be a direct cause of the achievement or failure to achieve organizational goals and objectives; can be internal or external

Monopolistic competition A market structure in which there are many firms offering slightly differentiated products and services

Monopoly A market structure in which there is only one seller of a product or provider of a service

Oligopoly A market structure in which there are only a few firms, whose products or services may be either differentiated or standardized

Participatory budget A budget that has been developed through a process of joint decision making by top management and operating personnel

Price elasticity of demand A relationship that reflects the percentage change in the quantity demanded relative to the percentage change in price for a good or service

Pure competition A market structure in which there are many firms, each with a small market share, producing identical products

Sales price variance The difference between actual and budgeted selling prices multiplied by the actual number of units sold

Sales volume variance The difference between actual and budgeted volumes multiplied by the budgeted selling price

Strategic planning The process of developing a statement of long-range goals for the organization and defining the strategies and policies that will help the organization achieve those goals

Substitute good A good that can be used in place of another to satisfy the same wants or needs

Tactical (or operational) planning The process of determining the specific objectives and means by which strategic plans will be achieved; also called operational planning

Zero-based budgeting A comprehensive budgeting process that systematically considers the priorities and alternatives for current and proposed activities in relation to organizational objectives (from **appendix**)

Lecture Outline

A. Purposes of Budgeting

1. The **budget** is the quantitative expression of an organization's commitment to planned activities and resource acquisition and use.

2. **Budgeting** The process of determining a financial plan for future operations. (see text **Exhibits 10-1 and 10-2**)

3. Budgets are a type of standard, and variances from budget can be computed.

4. Budgeting can help identify potential problems of achieving specified goals and objectives.

5. A well-prepared budget can be an effective device to communicate objectives, constraints, and expectations to people throughout an organization.

6. Managers must participate in the budgeting process in order to produce a spirit of cooperation.

7. Employee participation is needed to effectively integrate vital information from various sources as well as to obtain individual managerial commitment to the resulting budget.

8. The budget reflects the resource constraints under which managers must operate for the budget period ahead, so that the budget can be utilized as the basis for controlling activities and using resources.

9. The budgeting and planning processes are concerned with all organizational resources – (1) raw materials, (2) inventory, (3) supplies, (4) personnel, and (5) facilities; these processes can be viewed from a long-range or short-range perspective.

B. Strategic and Tactical Planning

1. **Strategic planning** is the process of developing a statement of long-range (five to ten years) goals for the organization and defining the strategies and policies that will help the organization achieve those goals.

2. A **key variable** is a critical factor believed to be a direct cause of the achievement or failure to achieve organizational goals and objectives; can be internal or external.

3. **Tactical (or operational) planning** is the process of determining the specific objectives and means by which strategic plans will be achieved; are short-term (one to eighteen months), single use plans that have been developed to address a given set of circumstances or for a specific time frame.

4. The annual budget is an example of a single use tactical plan; intermediate (quarterly and monthly) plans should also be included for the budget to work effectively.

5. Information regarding the economy, environment, technological developments, and available resources must be incorporated into the setting of goals and objectives for both strategic and tactical planning.

C. **Operating Environment**

1. The market structure in which a firm operates and the degree of competition it faces have a notable impact on the firm's ability to set strategic and tactical plans.

   a. **Pure competition** reflects a market structure in which there are many firms, each with small market share, producing identical products.

   b. **Monopolistic competition** involves a market structure in which there are many firms having slightly differentiated products and services.

   c. A **monopoly** is a market structure in which there is only one seller of a product or provider of a service.

   d. An **oligopoly** is a market structure in which there are only a few firms, whose products/services may be differentiated or standardized.

2. Governmental regulatory agencies monitor prices and trade practices on a fairly continuous basis to detect activities believed to be detrimental to healthy commerce.

3. Consumers are a major factor in a business' operating environment, and management needs market research to determine the factors that influence purchasers' rationale for paying certain prices.

   a. Most consumers must consider price in making a purchase because they are trying to make efficient use of their scarce resources.

   b. Consumers will seek similar products that meet their needs at lower prices if they think a product is priced too high. The consumers may seek alternatives if they do not find such similar products.

   c. **Price elasticity of demand** is a relationship that reflects the percentage change in the quantity demanded relative to the percentage change in price for a good or service. Demand for a product is said to be elastic with respect to price when consumer demand responds quickly and strongly to a change in price.

4. Buyers and sellers will both bid the price up when product demand exceeds product supply.

   a. A higher price often stimulates greater production, causing supply to increase (unless production is constrained by cost factors).

   b. Buyers and sellers will both bid the price down when product demand is less than product supply.

   c. A lower price should motivate lower production, which should lower supply.

   d. Supply and demand find a point at which they are equal as supply increases or decreases and demand increases or decreases due to changing prices.

D. **Product Life Cycle** (see text **Exhibit 10-7**)

   1. The specific product life cycle stages are: (1) development, (2) introduction, (3) growth, (4) maturity, and (5) harvest.

2. Companies must be aware of the stage its products are in since the stage may have a tremendous impact on costs, sales, and pricing strategies.

   a. Costs exist with no offsetting revenues in the development stage.

   b. Profits are still nonexistent during the introduction stage, since high costs are incurred and sales are just beginning.

   c. Costs tend to level off during the remaining three stages as standards are stabilized and production becomes routine.

   d. Sales increase through growth, level off in maturity, and then decline during the harvest stage.

3. Awareness of a forecasted selling price that the market will bear allows managers to determine a target production cost.

4. Decisions made during the design stage can affect product sales, design, costs, and quality for the remainder of the product's life cycle.

5. Products should be designed for the quality and cost desired.

6. Products need to be designed to use the fewest number of parts and parts should be standardized to the greatest extent possible.

7. Products should require only a minimal number of engineering changes after being released to production if they are designed properly during development.

8. A **substitute good** is a good that can be used in place of another to satisfy the same wants or needs.

   a. Sales during the introduction stage are usually quite low and selling prices often are set in some relationship to the market price of similar substitute goods or services, if such goods or services are available.

   b. Costs can be quite substantial in the introduction phase.

9. The growth stage begins when the product begins to break even.

   a. The product has been accepted by the market and profits begin to rise during the growth stage.

   b. Product quality may improve since competitors have improved on original production designs.

   c. Prices are fairly stable because many substitutes may exist or because consumers have become "attached" to the product and are willing to pay a particular price for it rather than buy a substitute.

10. Sales during the maturity stage begin to stabilize or slowly decline and firms often compete on the basis of selling price. Costs are often at their lowest level, so profits may be high.

11. The decline stage reflects waning sales, and prices are often cut dramatically to stimulate business.

12. Producers of goods and providers of services should be concerned with maximizing profits over a product's or service's life cycle because, to be profitable, revenues must be generated in excess of total product costs.

E. **Participation in the Budgeting Process**

   1. Budgeting activity should begin for future periods once management has decided upon the organization's strategic plan.

      a. The budgeting process requires the careful integration of a complex set of facts and projections with human relationships and attitudes.

      b. No one budgeting system is right for all organizations.

   2. Budgets can be derived in the following two ways:

      a. Budgets can be derived from the top down – an **imposed budget** is a budget that is prepared by top management with little or no input from operating personnel, who are simply informed of the budget goals and constraints.

      b. Budgets can be derived from the bottom up – a **participatory budget** is a budget that has been developed through a process of joint decision making by top management and operating personnel.

3. **Budget slack** is the intentional underestimation of revenues and/or overestimation of expenses, and may be introduced by managers.

   a. Slack may be built into the budget during the participation process; is not usually found in imposed budgets.

   b. A budget with slack allows subordinate managers to achieve their objectives with less effort than would be necessary if there was no slack.

   c. Budget slack creates problems due to the significant interaction of the budget factors.

4. Business budgets are usually prepared through a coordinated effort of input from operating personnel and revision by top management, so that the plans of all levels can be considered.

   a. Top management first sets strategic objectives for lower-level management; then, lower level managers suggest and justify their operations' performance targets.

   b. Upper-level managers combine all component budgets, evaluate the overall results, and provide feedback on any needed changes to the lower-level managers.

5. Management must review the complete budget before approving and implementing it to determine if the underlying assumptions on which the budget is based are reasonable.

   a. Budgeted figures are only as reasonable as the assumptions on which those figures are based.

   b. Management must then determine if the budgeted results are acceptable and realistic.

   c. Planned activities should be reconsidered and revised to more appropriately represent outcomes that were expressed during the tactical planning stage if the budget indicates that the results expected from planned activities do not achieve the desired objectives.

F. **The Budgeting Process**

  1. The budget is usually prepared on an annual basis and detailed by quarters, and then by months within those quarters. The *minimum* time to begin budget preparation is two to three months in advance of the period to be covered, but management must remember two things: (1) the development of a participatory budget will take longer than will an imposed budget, and (2) the larger and more complex the company is, the longer the budgeting will take.

  2. A **continuous (or rolling) budget** is an ongoing twelve-month budget that is created by successively adding a new budget month (twelve months into the future) as each current month expires.

  3. A **budget manual** is a detailed set of documents that provides information and guidelines about the budgetary process, and should include the following: (1) statements of the budgeting purpose and its desired results, (2) a listing of specific budgetary activities to be performed, (3) a calendar of scheduled budgetary activities, (4) sample budget forms, and (5) original, revised, and approved budgets.

G. **Budget Implementation and Control**

  1. A budget is implemented after it has been prepared and accepted.

  2. **Budget implementation** means that the budget is now considered a standard against which performance can be measured.

  3. Managers operating under budget guidelines should be provided copies of all appropriate budgets, and should be informed that managerial performance will be evaluated by comparing actual results to budgeted amounts. The evaluations should usually be made by budget category for specific time periods.

  4. The control phase begins once the budget is implemented.

  5. **Control** includes making actual-to-budget comparisons, determining variances, providing feedback to operating managers, investigating the causes of the variances, and taking any necessary corrective action. These activities indicate the cyclical nature of the budgeting process.

  6. Both positive and negative feedback are essential to the control process and must be provided in a timely manner to be useful.

7. Sales price and sales volume variances need to be analyzed.

   a. The **sales price variance** is the difference between actual and budgeted selling prices multiplied by the actual number of units sold.

   b. The **sales volume variance** is the difference between actual and budgeted volumes multiplied by the budgeted selling price.

8. Costs should be analyzed, using flexible budgets and flexible budget formulas, in relation to the actual sales volume rather than the budgeted sales volume.

   a. The comparison of actual expenses to budgeted expenses that were calculated at a different sales level will not provide valid information on how well costs were controlled during a period.

   b. Managers also need to analyze the ways in which money was spent. Such a spending analysis should focus on individual line items, not just totals, and on spending within categories.

   c. Income statement actual-to-budget comparisons are made in order to determine the underlying reasons for variances, requiring that the comparisons be made as early as possible.

9. Management should consider the effects that current changes in conditions may have on future operations and on the types and extent of future budgetary variances.

H. **Budget Revisions and Performance Evaluations**

   1. The budget, if actual performance is substantially less than expected, may or may not be revised depending on the causes of the variances.

   2. Budget revisions may be made if actual performance is substantially better than expected.

   3. Management should commend those responsible for positive performance, and should communicate the effects of such performance to related departments.

   4. Management must communicate to those persons being evaluated how or if budget revisions will affect performance evaluations when results do not turn out as expected.

5. Top management may want to compare performance to both the original and revised budgets and then use multiple evaluation tools to judge the quality as well as quantity of performance.

6. Budgetary slack can be reduced by evaluating actual performance against budgeted performance through a bonus system. Operating managers are rewarded with large bonuses for budgeting relatively high performance levels and achieving those levels.

7. Managers may play other "budget games." (see text **Exhibit 10-14**)

8. **Games** can be defined as a series of organized behavior patterns conforming to a set of rules that promote a defined outcome.

9. Budgets, to be effective in evaluating performance, should be challenging, but achievable.

I. **Budgeting in an International Business**

1. An organization in a multinational environment faces a virtually unlimited number of external variables that can affect the planning process.

2. Managers and employees should not be faulted for failing to achieve budget objectives if the fundamental causes reflect unforeseen, noncontrollable conditions.

J. **Zero-Based Budgeting – Appendix** (see text **Exhibit 10-15**)

1. Traditional budgeting is usually limited in its usefulness as a control tool, since poor budgeting techniques are often used.

2. **Appropriations** are maximum allowable expenditures for budget items.

3. **Zero-based budgeting (ZBB)** is a comprehensive budgeting process that systematically considers the priorities and alternatives for current and proposed activities in relation to organizational objectives.

a. Zero-based budgeting was originally developed for the government, and annual justification of programs and activities is required so that managers will rethink priorities within the context of agreed-upon objectives.

b. ZBB is applicable in all business organizations, especially in the support and service areas where non-monetary measures of performance are available.

c. ZBB does not provide measures of efficiency and is difficult to implement due to the significant amount of effort necessary to investigate the causes of prior costs and justify the purposes of budgeted costs.

4. The ZBB process includes three steps: (1) converting the company activities into decision packages, (2) ranking each decision package, and (3) allocating resources based on priorities.

Multiple Choice Questions from CMA Examinations

1. A continuous budget:
   a. drops the current month or quarter and adds a future month or a future quarter as the current month or quarter is completed.
   b. presents a statement of expectations for a period but does not present a firm commitment.
   c. presents the plan for only one level of activity and does not adjust to changes in the level of activity.
   d. presents the plan for a range of activity so that the plan can be adjusted to changes in activity.
   e. classifies budget requests by activity and estimates the benefits arising from each activity.

   The correct answer is a. (CMA June 1979, 4-7)

2. When comparing strategic planning with operational planning, which one of the following statements is most appropriate?
   a. Strategic planning is performed at all levels of management.
   b. Operational planning results in budget data.
   c. Strategic planning focuses on authority and responsibility.
   d. Operational planning is long-range in focus.
   e. Strategic planning is used in performance report preparation.

   The correct answer is b. (CMA June 1991, 3-7)

THE MASTER BUDGET

Learning Objectives

After reading and studying Chapter 11, you should be able to:

1. Determine the starting point of a master budget and why this item is chosen.

2. Prepare the various master budget schedules.

3. Relate the various master budget schedules to one another.

4. Understand why the cash budget is so important in the master budgeting process.

5. Relate the statement of cash flows to the income statement and the cash budget.

Terminology

Budget committee A group, usually composed of top management and the chief financial officer, that reviews and approves, or makes adjustments to, the master budget and/or the budgets submitted from operational managers

Capital budgeting The process of making decisions and budgeting for expenditures on long-term plant and equipment and investment items

Financial budget A budget that reflects the funds to be generated or used during the budget period; includes the cash and capital budgets and the projected or pro forma financial statements

Master budget The comprehensive set of all budgetary schedules and the pro forma financial statements of an organization

Operating budget A budget that is expressed in both units and dollars

Lecture Outline

A. **The Master Budget**

1. The **master budget** is the comprehensive set of all budgetary schedules and the pro forma financial statements of an organization.

    a. **Operating budgets** are budgets that are expressed in both units and dollars.

    b. **Financial budgets** are budgets that reflect the funds to be generated or used during the budget period; they include the cash and capital budgets and the projected or pro forma financial statements.

2. The output level of sales or service quantities that are selected for use in the master budget preparation affects all other organizational components; it is essential that all the components interact in a coordinated manner.

3. The budgetary process begins with the sales department's estimates of the types, quantities, and timing of demand for the company's products. (see text **Exhibit 11-1**)

B. **The Master Budget Illustrated** (see text **Exhibit 11-2**)

1. The **sales budget** is prepared by the Sales/Marketing Department and is demand driven. (See text **Exhibit 11-4**)

    a. The sales budget is prepared in terms of both units and sales dollars.

    b. Dollar sales figures are computed by multiplying sales quantities by product selling price.

2. The **production budget** follows naturally from the sales budget and uses the information regarding the type, quantity, and timing of units to be sold. (See text **Exhibit 11-5**)

    a. Sales information is combined with information on beginning and ending inventories so that managers can schedule the necessary production.

b. Ending inventory policy is generally specified by company management, and desired ending inventory is usually a function of the quantity and timing of demand in the upcoming period as related to the capacity and speed of the firm to produce goods.

3. The **purchases budget** for direct and indirect materials is prepared by the Purchasing Department. (see text **Exhibit 11-6**)

   a. The purchases budget is first stated in whole units of finished products.

   b. The budget is subsequently converted to individual direct material component requirements.

   c. The direct material component requirements are finally converted to cost of purchases figures.

4. The **direct labor budget** is prepared by the Personnel Department. (see text **Exhibit 11-7**)

   a. The labor budget reflects estimated factory direct labor costs that are based on standard hours of labor needed to produce the number of units shown in the production budget.

   b. Labor requirements are stated in ① total number of people, ② specific number of types of people, and ③ production hours needed for factory employees.

5. The **factory overhead budget** is prepared by Operations Management. (see text **Exhibit 11-8**)

   a. Overhead is another production cost that management must estimate.

   b. All overhead costs must be specified, and mixed costs must be separated into their fixed and variable components.

6. The **selling, general, and administrative expenses budget** is prepared by administrative and sales staffs. (see text **Exhibit 11-9**)

   a. The operating expenses for each month can be predicted in the same fashion as overhead costs.

   b. Sales figures rather than production levels are used as the measure of activity in preparing this budget.

7. The **capital budget** is prepared by Capital Facilities Management. (see text **Exhibit 11-10**)

   a. **Capital budgeting** is the process of making decisions and budgeting for expenditures on long-term plant and equipment and investment items.

   b. The capital budget is prepared separately from the master budget, and capital budgeting does not affect the master budgeting process.

8. The **cash budget** is prepared by the Treasurer. (see text **Exhibits 11-12, 11-13, and 11-14**)

   a. A cash budget can be constructed after all the preceding budgets have been developed.

   b. Cash budgets can be used ① to predict seasonal fluctuations in any potential cash flow, indicating a need for short-term borrowing and a potential schedule of repayments; ② to show the possibility of surplus cash that could be used for investment; and ③ to measure the performance of the accounts receivable and accounts payable departments by comparing actual to scheduled collections, payments, and discounts taken.

   c. Managers translate sales revenue information into actual cash receipts through the use of an expected collection pattern; the balances of the Accounts Receivable and Allowance for Uncollectibles accounts can be projected once such a schedule of cash collections has been prepared.

   d. Management can prepare an estimated cash disbursements schedule for accounts payable using the purchases information.

   e. The cash receipts and disbursements information is used to prepare the cash budget.

9. The **budgeted financial statements** are prepared by the Accounting Department.

   a. The budgeted financial statements for the period reflect the results that will be achieved if the estimates and assumptions used for all previous budgets actually occur.

   b. The statements allow management to determine if the predicted results are acceptable for the period.

c. Management has the opportunity to change and adjust items before beginning the new period if the predicted results are not acceptable.

d. Management must prepare a **cost of goods manufactured schedule,** which is necessary to determine cost of goods sold, before an income statement can be drafted. (see text **Exhibit 11-15**)

e. The budgeted **income statement** uses much of the information previously developed in determining the revenues and expenses for the period. (see text **Exhibit 11-16**)

f. The pro forma **balance sheet** can be prepared upon completion of the income statement. (see text **Exhibit 11-17**)

g. The information found on the income statement, balance sheet, and cash budget is used in preparing a **statement of cash flows (SCF)**. The SCF explains the change in the cash balance by reflecting the company's sources and uses of cash.

C. Concluding Comments

1. Demand must be predicted as accurately and with as many details as is possible because of its fundamental nature in the budgeting process.

   a. Sales forecasts must indicate the type and quantity of products to be sold, geographic locations of sales, types of buyers, and points in time that sales are to be made.

   b. Such detail is necessary because ① different products require different production and distribution facilities; ② different customers have different credit terms and payment schedules; and ③ different seasons or months may necessitate different shipping schedules or methods.

2. Estimated sales demand has a pervasive impact on the master budget.

   a. Managers use as much information as is available and may combine several estimation approaches in arriving at a valid prediction.

   b. The combining of prediction methods helps corroborate estimates and reduces managerial uncertainty.

3. Ways of estimating future demand are: (1) asking sales personnel for a subjective consensus, (2) making simple extrapolations of past trends, (3) using market research, and (4) employing statistical and other mathematical models.

4. The master budget can and should be used for a variety of purposes, such as (1) to help obtain bank loans and (2) to monitor performance by comparing budgeted figures to actual results.

Multiple Choice Questions from CMA Examinations

Questions 1 through 4 are based on Kelly Company, which is a retail sporting goods store that uses accrual accounting for its records. Facts regarding Kelly's operations are as follows:

- Sales are budgeted at $220,000 for December 1994 and $200,000 for January 1995.
- Collections are expected to be 60% in the month of sale and 38% in the month following the sale.
- Gross margin is 25% of sales.
- A total of 80% of the merchandise held for resale is purchased in the month prior to the month of sale and 20% is purchased in the month of sale. Payment for merchandise is made in the month following the purchase.
- Other expected monthly expenses to be paid in cash are $22,600.
- Annual depreciation is $216,000.

Below is Kelly Company's statement of financial position at November 30, 1994.

Assets

Cash	$ 22,000
Accounts receivable (net of $4,000 allowance for uncollectible accounts)	76,000
Inventory	132,000
Property, plant, and equipment (net of $680,000 accumulated depreciation)	870,000
Total assets	$ 1,100,000

Liabilities and Stockholders' Equity

Accounts payable	$ 162,000
Common stock	800,000
Retained earnings	138,000
Total liabilities and stockholders' equity	$ 1,100,000

1. The budgeted cash collections for December 1994 are:
   a. $208,000.
   b. $132,000.
   c. $203,600.
   d. $212,000.
   e. some amount other than those given above.

The correct answer is a. (CMA December 1983, 4-22)

Solution

Accounts receivable	$ 76,000
December sales of $220,000 X 60%	132,000
Budgeted cash collections	$ 208,000

2. The pro forma income <loss> before income taxes for December 1994 is:
   a. $32,400.
   b. $28,000.
   c. $14,400.
   d. $10,000.
   e. some amount other than those given above.

   The correct answer is d. (CMA December 1983, 4-23)

Solution

Sales	$ 220,000
Cost of sales	<165,000>
Gross margin	$ 55,000
Cash operating expenses	< 22,600>
Depreciation expense	< 18,000>
Bad debts expense	< 4,400>
Net income	$ 10,000

3. The projected balance in accounts payable on December 31, 1994 is:

   a. $162,000.
   b. $204,000.
   c. $153,000.
   d. $160,000.
   e. some amount other than those given above.

   The correct answer is c. (CMA December 1983, 4-24)

Solution

Accounts payable at December 1, 1994	$ 162,000
December purchases	153,000
December payments	<162,000>
Accounts payable at December 31, 1994	$ 153,000

4. The projected balance in inventory on December 31, 1994 is:
   a. $160,000.
   b. $120,000.
   c. $153,000.
   d. $150,000.
   e. some amount other than those given above.

The correct answer is b. (CMA December 1983, 4-25)

Solution

Inventory at December 1, 1994	$ 132,000
December purchases	153,000
December cost of sales	<165,000>
Inventory at December 31, 1994	$ 120,000

Questions 5 and 6 concern Pardise Company, which budgets on an annual basis for its fiscal year. The following beginning and ending inventory levels (in units) are planned for the fiscal year of July 1, 1995 through June 30, 1996.

	July 1, 1995	June 30, 1996
Raw material*	40,000	50,000
Work in process	10,000	10,000
Finished goods	80,000	50,000

* Two (2) units of raw material are needed to produce each unit of finished product.

5. If Pardise Company plans to sell 480,000 units during the 1995-96 fiscal year, the number of units it would have to manufacture during the year would be:
   a. 440,000 units.
   b. 480,000 units.
   c. 510,000 units.
   d. 450,000 units.
   e. some amount other than those given above.

The correct answer is d. (CMA June 1986, 4-26)

Solution

Units:

To be sold	480,000
Desired ending inventory	50,000
Total required	530,000
Desired beginning inventory	< 80,000>
To be produced	450,000

6. If 500,000 finished units were to be manufactured during the 1995-96 fiscal year by Pardise Company, the units of raw material needed to be purchased would be:

a. 1,000,000 units.

b. 1,020,000 units.

c. 1,010,000 units.

d.   990,000 units.

e. some amount other than those given above.

The correct answer is c. (CMA June 1986, 4-27)

Solution

Units:

Required for production	1,000,000
Desired ending inventory	50,000
Total required	1,050,000
Desired beginning inventory	< 40,000>
To be purchased	1,010,000

CONTROLLING NONINVENTORY COSTS

Learning Objectives

After reading and studying Chapter 12, you should be able to:

1. Recognize why cost consciousness is of great importance to all members of an organization.

2. Differentiate between committed and discretionary costs.

3. Understand how the benefits from discretionary cost expenditures can be measured.

4. Determine when standards are applicable to discretionary costs.

5. Explain how a budget helps in controlling discretionary costs.

6. (Appendix) Understand how program budgeting is used for cost control in not-for-profit entities.

Terminology

Committed cost The cost of the basic plant assets and personnel structure that an organization must have to operate

Cost avoidance A process of finding acceptable alternatives to high-cost items and not spending money for unnecessary goods or services

Cost consciousness A companywide employee attitude toward cost understanding, cost containment, cost avoidance, and cost reduction

Cost containment The process of attempting, to the extent possible, to minimize period-by-period increases in per-unit variable and total fixed costs

Cost control system A logical structure of formal and informal activities designed to influence costs and to enable management to analyze and evaluate how well expenditures were managed during a period

Cost reduction A process of lowering current costs, especially those in excess of necessary costs

Discretionary cost An optional cost that a decision maker must periodically review to determine whether it continues to be in accord with ongoing policies

Effectiveness A measure of how well the firm's objectives and goals were achieved; it involves comparing actual output results with desired results

Efficiency The degree to which the relationship between outputs and inputs is satisfactory

Engineered cost Any cost that has been found to bear an observable and known relationship to a quantifiable activity base

Horizontal price fixing A practice by which competitors attempt to regulate prices through an agreement or conspiracy

Price fixing A practice by which firms conspire to set a product's price at a specified level

Program budgeting An approach to budgeting that relates resource inputs to service outputs and thereby focuses on the relationship of benefits to cost expenditures (from **appendix**)

Strategic staffing A practice in which departments analyze their personnel needs by considering long-term objectives and determine a specific combination of permanent and temporary or highly-skilled and less-skilled employees that offer the best opportunity to meet those needs

Vertical price fixing Collusion between producing businesses and their distributors to control the prices at which their products may be sold to consumers

Lecture Outline

A. Cost Control Systems

1. A **cost control system** is a logical structure of formal and informal activities designed to influence costs and to enable management to analyze and evaluate how well expenditures were managed during a period.

2. An effective cost control system should provide three functions: (1) control before an event, (2) control during an event, and (3) control after an event. (see text **Exhibit 12-1**)

3. An event could be (1) a period of time, (2) the production of a product, or (3) the performance of a service.

4. **Cost consciousness** is a companywide employee attitude toward cost understanding, cost containment, cost avoidance, and cost reduction. (see text **Exhibit 12-2**)

5. Cost control is first exercised when the budget is prepared, but budgets can be properly prepared only when the reasons for periodic cost changes are understood and cost control can be achieved only with an understanding of *why* costs may differ from the budgeted amounts.

   a. A flexible budget can compensate for changes in variable costs due to activity level changes by providing expected variable costs at the actual activity level.

   b. Managers can subsequently make valid budget-to-actual cost comparisons to determine if total variable costs were properly controlled.

   c. The following factors can also cause costs to differ from prior periods or the budget: ① cost changes due to inflation/deflation, ② cost changes due to technological advances, ③ cost changes due to supply and demand, ④ cost changes due to tax or regulatory adjustments, ⑤ cost changes due to quantity of competition, ⑥ cost changes due to seasonality or other timing factors, or ⑦ cost changes due to quantity purchased.

6. **Price fixing** is a practice by which firms conspire to set a product's price at a specified level.

   a. **Vertical price fixing** involves collusion between producing businesses and their distributors to control the prices at which their products may be sold to consumers; is also known as resale price maintenance.

   b. **Horizontal price fixing** is a practice by which competitors attempt to regulate prices through an agreement or conspiracy.

7. **Cost containment** is the processing of attempting, to the extent possible, to minimize period-by-period increases in per-unit variable and total fixed costs.

   a. Cost containment is difficult for changes due to ① inflation/deflation, ② technological advances, ③ supply and demand, or ④ tax or regulatory adjustments since these factors exist outside the organizational structure.

   b. Managers may be able to practice cost avoidance in hopes of minimizing the effects that these causes have on the organization's costs.

   c. Costs that rise due to ① quantity of competition, ② seasonality or other timing factors, or ③ quantity purchased are subject to cost containment activities.

8. **Cost avoidance** is a process of finding acceptable alternatives to high-cost items and not spending money for unnecessary goods or services. A cost avoidance attitude should have managers and employees seeking to eliminate unnecessary expenditures.

9. **Cost reduction** is a process of lowering current costs, especially those in excess of what is necessary.

   a. Cost reduction often focuses on the activities that are causing costs to occur.

   b. Corresponding costs will be reduced or eliminated if non-value-added activities can be reduced or eliminated.

   c. Many companies believe that the elimination of jobs and labor is an effective way to reduce costs, but cutting costs by cutting people sometimes creates other problems.

d. **Strategic staffing** represents a practice in which departments analyze their personnel needs by considering long-term objectives and determine a specific combination of permanent and temporary or highly-skilled and less-skilled employees that offer the best opportunity to meet those needs.

e. Cost reduction is possible by using part-time rather than full-time employees or external providers of services rather than maintaining internal departments.

f. Managers set the tone for the department or organization by projecting cost-conscious attitudes.

g. Employees usually do not mind engaging in cost control efforts if such efforts will provide the employees some benefit either monetarily or at performance review time.

h. Most companies that institute employee suggestion programs find that employees are able to contribute significantly to improvement ideas.

10. Managers should use the following five-step method of implementing a cost control system.

a. First – the types of costs incurred by an organization must be understood.

b. Second – the need for cost consciousness must be communicated to all employees for it to be effective.

c. Third – employees must be motivated by education and incentives to embrace the concepts, and managers must be flexible enough to allow for changes from the current method of operation.

d. Fourth – reports must be generated that indicate actual results, budget-to-actual comparisons, and variances.

e. Fifth – the cost control system should be viewed as a long-run process, not a short-run solution.

B. Committed Fixed Costs

1. All fixed costs (and the activities that create them) can be categorized as either committed or discretionary, and the difference between the two categories is primarily the time horizon for which management binds itself to the activity and the cost.

2. **Committed costs** are the costs associated with basic plant assets or with the personnel structure that an organization must have to operate.

3. Control of committed costs is first provided during the evaluation process of comparing the expected benefits derived from plant assets (or human resources) to the expected costs of such investments.

4. Managers must decide which activities are necessary to attain company objectives and determine which assets are needed to support those activities.

C. Discretionary Costs

1. **Discretionary costs** are the optional costs that a decision maker must periodically review to determine whether such costs continue to be in accordance with ongoing policies.

2. A discretionary cost is a fixed cost that reflects a management decision to fund an activity at a specified amount for a specified time period, and the decision to fund an activity as discretionary is based on organizational policy or management preference.

3. Advertising, public relations, employee development programs, and research and development are common examples of discretionary costs, but there are no specific activities whose costs will consistently, in all organizations, be considered discretionary.

4. Managers believe, in the short run, that discretionary cost reductions can be made without impairing the organization's long-range profitability or capacity.

5. Discretionary cost activities vary in type and magnitude from one day to the next, and the output quality of discretionary cost activities may also vary according to the tasks and skill levels of the persons performing those activities.

6. Discretionary costs therefore are not normally susceptible to the precise planning and control measures available for variable production costs or the cost/benefit analysis techniques available to control committed fixed costs.

7. Company goals must be translated into specific objectives and policies that will lead to organizational success before top management can budget amounts for discretionary cost activities.

8. Management generally does not know how much discretionary cost is the optimal amount for the activity involved, so discretionary cost appropriations are usually based on three factors: (1) the activity's perceived significance to the achievement of objectives and goals, (2) the upcoming period's expected level of operations, and (3) managerial negotiations in the budgetary process.

9. Managers are expected to spend the full amount of their appropriations within the specified time frame for some discretionary costs, while the "less is better" adage is appropriate for others.

10. Managers often view discretionary activities and costs as though they are committed, but such a viewpoint does not change the underlying discretionary nature of the item. Top management must, in such circumstances, have a great deal of faith in the ability of lower-level management to perform the specified tasks in an efficient manner.

11. The amounts spent on discretionary activities are the inputs to a process that should provide some desired monetary or surrogate output.

    a. Comparisons of input costs and output results may be used to determine if a reasonable cost/benefit relationship exists between the two.

    b. Managers, if possible, evaluate the cost/benefit relationship by how efficiently costs were used and how effectively those costs achieved their purposes.

    c. Many discretionary costs cannot be closely tied to outcomes because: ① several years may transpire before the output of a discretionary activity is noticeable, and ② it is often virtually impossible to be certain that a cause-and-effect relationship exists between discretionary cost inputs and particular outputs.

12. **Efficiency** is the degree to which the relationship between outputs and inputs is satisfactory.

13. **Effectiveness** is a measure of how well the firm's objectives and goals were achieved; it involves comparing actual output results with desired results.

D. Controlling Discretionary Costs

1. **Engineered costs** are any costs that have been found to bear an observable and known relationship to a quantifiable activity base; an engineered cost can be treated as a variable, rather than a fixed, cost.

2. Discretionary cost activities that can be categorized as engineered costs are normally geared to a performance measure relative to work accomplished.

3. Monetary control is effected through the use of budget-to-actual comparisons once discretionary cost appropriations have been made.

4. Actual results are compared to expected results and explanations should be provided for the variances.

5. Effective cost consciousness can help provide valid explanations for variances.

E. Controlling Quality Costs

1. A discretionary cost category that is often mentioned is that of quality assurance and quality control.

2. Quality costs are difficult to reduce in the short-term without harming the long term profitability potential of an organization, due to the current competitive business emphasis on TQM.

3. Noncompliance costs are considered failure costs and result from production or service imperfections.

   a. The costs in this category are equal to ① all internal failure costs (including scrap and rework) plus ② all external failure costs (including product returns due to quality problems, warranty costs, and complaint department costs).

   b. The amount of failure costs is reduced by expenditures made for either prevention or appraisal.

4. Quality costs have not been recognized in the accounting system.

5. An organization must first be able to calculate its total cost of quality in order to attempt to control the cost of quality. Quality costs should be measured as accurately as is possible and practical, and the benefits of those costs estimated.

6. High quality provides a company the ability to improve current profits — either by (1) controlling failure costs (2) by selling additional product, or, if the market will bear, (3) by charging higher prices.

7. Overall costs should decline and productivity should increase when quality is increased through greater attention to prevention and appraisal activities.

   a. Lower costs and greater productivity support lower prices which, in turn, usually stimulates demand.

   b. Greater market is the result — meaning that surrogate measures like fewer customer returns can be translated into monetary measures of profit increases.

F. **Program Budgeting — Appendix**

   1. **Program budgeting** is an approach to budgeting that relates resource inputs to service outputs and thereby focuses on the relationship of benefits to cost expenditures.

   2. Program budgeting is useful for cost control purposes in certain types of organizations: (1) Governmental organizations, (2) not-for-profit organizations, and (3) service activities in for-profit businesses.

   3. Program budgeting starts by defining objectives in terms of output results rather than quantity of input activities.

      a. Effectiveness can be measured once output results have been defined in some measurable terms.

      b. A thorough analysis of alternative activities to achieve a firm's objectives is necessary, and includes the projection of both quantitative and qualitative costs and benefits for each alternative and the selection of those alternatives that, in top management's judgment, yield a satisfactory result at a reasonable cost.

      c. The choices are translated into budget appropriations to be acted on by the manager responsible for the related programs.

4. Detailed surrogate measures of output must be used, necessitating that the following questions be answered:

   a. When should results be measured?

   b. What results should be chosen as output measures?

   c. What program actually caused the result?

   d. Did the program actually impact the target population?

Multiple Choice Questions from CMA Examinations

1. Committed costs are:
   a. those management decides to incur in the current period to enable the company to achieve objectives other than the filling of orders placed by customers.
   b. likely to respond to the amount of attention devoted to them by a specified manager.
   c. governed mainly by past decisions that established the current levels of operating and organizational capacity and that only change slowly in response to small changes in capacity.
   d. those that fluctuate in total in response to small changes in the rate of use of capacity.
   e. amortized costs that were capitalized in previous periods.

   The correct answer is c. (CMA June 1978, 4-10)

2. Discretionary costs are:
   a. those management decides to incur in the current period to enable the company to achieve objectives other than the filling of orders placed by customers.
   b. likely to respond to the amount of attention devoted to them by a specified manager.
   c. governed mainly by past decisions that established the current levels of operating and organizational capacity and that only change slowly in response to small changes in capacity.
   d. amortized costs that were capitalized in previous periods.
   e. unaffected by current managerial decisions.

   The correct answer is a. (CMA June 1978, 4-11)

CONTROLLING INVENTORY AND PRODUCTION COSTS

Learning Objectives

After reading and studying Chapter 13, you should be able to:

1. Understand why managers use ABC inventory control systems.

2. Calculate and use economic order quantity and reorder point.

3. Understand why a company carries safety stock and how the appropriate amount is estimated.

4. Differentiate between the economic order quantity model and material requirements planning.

5. Evaluate the workings of the push and pull systems of production control.

6. Explain the JIT philosophy and how it affects production.

7. Explain how the traditional accounting system would change if a JIT inventory system were adopted.

8. Explain the impact of FMS on production and on satisfying customers.

Terminology

ABC analysis An inventory control method that separates items into three groups based on annual cost-to-volume usage; items having the highest dollar volume are referred to as A items, while C items represent the lowest dollar volume

Backflush costing A costing system that focuses on output and works backward through the system to allocate costs to cost of goods sold and inventory

Bottleneck Any resource whose ability to process is less than the need for processing

Carrying cost The variable cost of carrying one unit of inventory in stock for one year; consists of storage, handling, insurance charges, property taxes based on inventory size, possible losses obsolescence or the like, and opportunity cost

Computer integrated manufacturing (CIM) A production system in which two or more flexible manufacturing systems are connected by a host computer and an information network

Economic order quantity (EOQ) An estimate of the least costly number of units per order that would provide the optimal balance between ordering and carrying costs

Economic production run (EPR) The quantity of units to produce that minimizes the total cost of setting up a production run and carrying costs

Just-in-time (JIT) manufacturing system A production system with the goals of acquiring components and producing inventory units only as they are needed, minimizing product defects, and reducing lead and setup times for acquisition and production

Kanban The Japanese word for card; another name for just-in-time manufacturing which originated in Japan from the use of cards to control the flow of materials or units between work centers

Lead time The time from the placement of an order to the arrival of the goods

Manufacturing cells Linear or U-shaped grouping of workers and/or machines

Manufacturing resource planning (MRP II) A fully integrated computer simulation system that involves the functional areas of marketing, finance, and manufacturing in planning the master production schedule using the MRP method; also can calculate resource needs such as labor and machine hours

Material requirements planning (MRP) A computer simulation system that helps companies plan by coordinating future production output requirements with individual future production input needs using a master production schedule (MPS)

Order point The inventory level that triggers the placement of an order

Ordering cost The variable costs associated with preparing, receiving, and paying for an order

Pull system A production system in which parts are delivered or manufactured only as they are needed

Purchasing cost The quoted purchase price minus any discounts allowed plus shipping charges

Push system A production system in which work centers may produce inventory that is not currently needed because of lead time or economic order (or production) quantity requirements; the excess inventory is stored until it is needed

Red-line system An inventory system in which a single container (or stack) of inventory is available for production needs and a red line is painted on the inventory container (or on the wall, for a stack) at a point deemed to be the reorder point

Safety stock The quantity of inventory kept on hand by a company to compensate for potential fluctuations in usage or unusual delays in lead time

Setup cost The direct and indirect labor cost of getting equipment ready for a new production run

Stockout A condition in which a company does not have inventory available when customers request it or when it is needed for production

Throughput A plant's output to customers during a single period

Two-bin system An inventory system in which two containers or stacks of inventory are available for production needs; when production begins to use materials in the second bin, a purchase order is placed to refill the first bin

Lecture Outline

A. MANAGING INVENTORY

1. **ABC analysis** is an inventory control method that separates items into three groups based on annual cost-to-volume usage. (see text **Exhibit 13-1**)

   a. Items having the highest dollar volume are referred to as A items, while C items represent the lowest dollar volume.

   b. Management can determine the best inventory control method for each item once inventory is categorized as an A, B, or C item.

2. Under a **two-bin system**, two containers or stacks of inventory are available for production needs; when production begins to use materials in the second bin, a purchase order is placed to refill the first bin.

3. In a **red-line system**, a single container (or stack) of inventory is available for production needs; a red line is painted on the inventory container (or on the wall for a stack) at a point deemed to be the reorder point.

B. COSTS ASSOCIATED WITH INVENTORY (see text **Exhibit 13-2**)

1. Most organizations that engage in any type of conversion use inputs and produce outputs that are tangible or physical in nature.

   a. Inputs or outputs that have a physical presence can be stored or inventoried.

   b. Non-physical inputs or outputs, such as direct labor or cleaning services, are simultaneously consumed as they are supplied.

2. Good inventory management mostly relies on cost-minimizing strategies; there are four basic costs associated with inventory:
   (1) purchasing/production, (2) ordering, (3) carrying goods in stock, and (4) not carrying goods in stock.

3. The **purchasing cost** of inventory is the quoted purchase price minus any discounts allowed plus shipping charges.

4. **Ordering costs** are the variable costs associated with preparing, receiving, and paying for an order.

   a. Ordering costs include the cost of forms and a variety of clerical costs.

   b. Such costs are traditionally expensed as incurred, but the costs could be traced to the items ordered as an additional direct cost under an activity-based costing system.

   c. Retailers incur ordering costs for all their merchandise inventory, while manufacturing companies incur ordering costs for raw material purchases.

5. **Set-up costs** are the direct and indirect labor costs of getting equipment ready for each new production run and are incurred in lieu of ordering costs.

6. Inventory **carrying costs** are the variable costs of carrying one unit of inventory in stock for one year; consist of storage, handling, insurance charges, property taxes based on inventory size, possible losses from obsolescence or the like, and opportunity cost.

7. A **stockout** is the condition in which a company does not have inventory available when customers request it or when it is needed for production. Stockout cost is not easily determinable or recordable, but includes: (1) lost customer goodwill, (2) lost contribution margin from being unable to fill a sale, and (3) the ordering and shipping charges incurred from filling special orders.

C. SUPPLIERS AND QUANTITIES

1. Purchase cost must be viewed in relation to quality and reliability, and the supplier with the lowest cost is not necessarily the best supplier.

2. The objective of the purchase manager is to buy in the most economical quantity possible, which requires consideration of the inventory ordering and carrying costs.

3. The **economic order quantity (EOQ)** is an estimate of the least costly number of units per order that would provide the optimal balance between ordering and carrying costs.

a. The EOQ formula is:

$$EOQ = \sqrt{\frac{2QO}{C}}$$

where
EOQ = economic order quantity in units
Q = estimated quantity used per year in units
O = estimated cost of placing *one* order
C = estimated cost to carry *one* unit in stock for one year

b. The EOQ formula does not include purchase cost since that amount relates to the decision of "from whom to buy" rather than to "how many to buy."

c. Purchase cost does not affect ordering and carrying costs, except to the extent that opportunity cost is calculated on the basis of investment.

4. The EOQ model assumes that orders will be filled exactly when needed, so that the inventory on hand will be zero units when an order arrives.

a. The average inventory is therefore half of any given order size.

b. The number of times an order must be placed depends on how many units are ordered each time, and total number of orders equals total annual quantity of units needed divided by the size of each order placed.

5. The EOQ formula contains *estimated* values, but small cost estimation errors usually will not cause a major impact on total cost.

6. Factors like cash availability and storage space constraints should be considered if the cost of ordering quantities close to the EOQ level is not significantly different from the cost of ordering at the EOQ level.

7. An **economic production run (EPR)** is the quantity of units to produce that minimizes the total costs of setting up a production run and carrying costs. (see text **Footnote 7**)

    a. The EPR formula:

$$EPR = \sqrt{\frac{2QS}{C}}$$

    where   EPR = economic production run
                   Q = estimated quantity used per year in units
                   S = estimated cost of setting up *one* production run
                   C = estimated cost to carry *one* unit in stock for one year

    b. The differences in costs among various run sizes around the EPR may not be significant, and if such costs are insignificant, management would have a range of acceptable, economical production run quantities.

8. The **order point** is the inventory level that triggers the placement of an order.

9. **Lead time** is the time from the placement of an order to the arrival of the goods. The order point with lead time is calculated as:

    Order Point = Daily Usage X Lead Time

10. **Safety stock** is the quantity of inventory kept on hand by a company to compensate for potential fluctuating usage or unusual delays in lead time. When a safety stock is maintained, the order point formula is:

    Order Point = (Daily Usage X Lead Time) + Safety Stock

    a. A safety stock of inventory is carried to act as a buffer to protect the company against the possibility of stockouts. A simple way to estimate safety stock is as follows:

        Safety Stock = (Maximum Usage - Normal Usage) X Lead Time

    b. Mathematical determination of EOQ and optimal safety stock will help a company control its investment in inventory, but such models are only as reliable as the estimates used in the formula.

D. MATERIALS REQUIREMENTS PLANNING

1. **Materials requirements planning (MRP)** is a computer simulation system that helps companies plan by coordinating future production output requirements with individual future production input needs using a master production schedule (MPS).

   a. MRP was developed to answer the questions of what items are needed, how many of them are needed, and when they are needed.

   b. The MRP computer model, which is similar to a production budget, accesses the product's bill of materials to determine all production components once projected sales and production for a product have been estimated.

   c. Needed quantities are compared to current inventory balances and, if purchases are necessary, the estimated lead times for each purchase are accessed.

   d. The model will then generate a time-sequenced schedule for purchases and production component needs.

   e. The process is designed so that when the program is run several times all potential bottlenecks are identified and compensated for. A **bottleneck** is any resource whose ability to process is less than the need for processing.

2. **Manufacturing resource planning (MRP II)** is a fully integrated computer simulation system that involves the functional areas of marketing, finance, and manufacturing in planning the MPS using the MRP method; also can calculate resource needs such as labor and machine hours.

3. The MRP models extend, rather than eliminate, the EOQ concept.

   a. MRP indicates which items of inventory to order at what points in time.

   b. A **push system** is a production system in which work centers may produce inventory that is not currently needed because of lead time or economic order (or production) quantity requirements; the excess inventory is stored until it is needed. (see text **Exhibit 13-4**)

4. MRP and MRP II have their problems, some of which are caused by their less-than-realistic underlying assumptions.

E. **Just-in-Time Systems**

1. The **just-in-time (JIT) philosophy** is applicable in any type of organization; the basic purpose of the philosophy is to minimize wasted activities and excess costs. (see text **Exhibit 13-5**)

2. A **JIT manufacturing system** is a production system with the goals of acquiring components and producing inventory units only as they are needed, minimizing product defects, and reducing lead and setup times for acquisition and production.

3. A JIT system always has three primary goals: (1) elimination of any production process or operation that does not add value to the product/service, (2) continuously improving production/performance efficiency, and (3) reducing the total cost of production/performance while increasing quality.

4. **Kanban** is the Japanese word for card or *ticket*; another name for JIT manufacturing which originated in Japan from the use of cards to control the flow of materials or units between work centers.

5. A **pull system** is a production system in which parts are delivered or manufactured only as they are needed. (see text **Exhibit 13-7**)

   a. JIT is a pull system; therefore, forecasted sales demand is the controlling production force.

   b. The production schedule is set for an extended period (like a month), once demand is estimated, and schedule changes should be minimal.

6. The most impressive results from JIT are usually reached only after the system has been operational for five to ten years.

7. A primary objective of JIT is reduction of setup time which allows processing to rapidly shift among different types of units.

   a. Increases in initial setup time and cost have been found to be more than recovered by the savings from reduction of downtime, work in process inventory, and materials handling as well as increasing safety, flexibility, and ease of operation.

b. Companies implementing such procedures use many low-cost rapid setups rather than using the traditional approach of a small number of expensive setups; setup cost is considered to be almost totally variable rather than fixed.

8. The implementation of high quality standards that result in zero quality errors is another essential part of JIT product processing.

9. The physical plant is arranged in a way that is conducive to the flow of goods and the organization of workers in an effective JIT system.

   a. Streamlined design allows more visual controls to be instituted for problems such as excess inventory, product defects, equipment malfunctions, and out-of-place tools.

   b. **Manufacturing cells** are linear or U-shaped groupings of workers and/or machines which serve to minimize time and cost through the plant. The cells ① reduce inventory storage, ② improve materials handling and flow, ③ increase machine utilization rates, maximize communication among workers, and result in better quality control.

10. The employee empowerment concept is an underlying feature of a JIT system.

    a. Companies may find that workers, by knowing more about the entire process, are better able to provide constructive suggestions about process improvement.

    b. The JIT philosophy is more than just a cost cutting endeavor or a means of reducing personnel, and it requires effective human resource management as well as a dedication to teamwork.

F. **Accounting Implications of JIT**

1. Variance reporting and analysis virtually disappear in JIT systems.

   a. Material price variances should be minimal due to long-term price agreements with vendors.

   b. The ability to control materials quality is provided by the ongoing use of specified vendors, so that little or no material usage variances should be caused by substandard materials.

    c. The JIT system is halted when defects are encountered and the error causing an unfavorable materials usage variance is corrected.

    d. Labor variances should be minimal if standard rates and times have been appropriately set.

    e. A JIT system reemphasizes that variances should be determinable on the spot so that causes can be ascertained and, if possible, promptly removed.

    f. Direct labor and factory overhead costs should be recorded in a Conversion Costs Control account under JIT.

    g. Companies adopting a JIT system no longer need a separate raw materials or stores control inventory classification; JIT companies should use a Raw and in Process Materials account.

2. **Backflush costing** is a costing system that focuses on output and works backward through the system to allocate costs to cost of goods sold and inventory.

    a. **Throughput** is the output of a plant to the customer during a single period.

    b. Fewer costs will need to be arbitrarily allocated to products since more costs can be traced directly to their related output.

G. **Flexible Manufacturing Systems and Computer Integrated Manufacturing**

1. A **flexible manufacturing system (FMS)** is a network of robots and material conveyance devices monitored and controlled by computers that allows for rapid production and prompt responsiveness to changes in production needs.

2. **Computer integrated manufacturing (CIM)** is the integration of two or more flexible manufacturing systems through the use of a host computer and an information networking system.

H. **Journal Entries for Backflush Costing** (see text **Exhibit 13-12**)

Multiple Choice Questions from CMA Examinations

1. Which of the following items is not included in the annual carrying costs of inventory?
   a. Cost of capital.
   b. Insurance on inventory.
   c. Annual warehouse depreciation.
   d. Taxes on inventory.
   e. Inventory breakage on stored inventory.

   The correct answer is c. (CMA December 1983, 5-22)

2. Which of the following items is irrelevant for a company that is attempting to minimize the cost of a stockout?
   a. Cost of placing an order.
   b. Contribution margin on lost sales.
   c. Storage cost of inventory.
   d. Size of the safety stock.
   e. Probability of being out of stock.

   The correct answer is a. (CMA December 1983, 5-24)

Questions 3 through 5 are based on Gerstein Company, which manufactures a line of deluxe office fixtures. The annual demand for its miniature oak file is estimated to be 5,000 units. The annual cost of carrying one unit in inventory is $10, and the cost to initiate a production run is $1,000. There are no miniature oak files on hand, and Gerstein has scheduled four equal production runs of the miniature oak file for the coming year, the first of which is to be run immediately. Gerstein has 250 business days per year. Assume that sales occur uniformly throughout the year and that production is instantaneous.

3. If Gerstein Company does not maintain a safety stock, the estimated total carrying costs for the miniature oak files for the coming year is:
   a. $ 5,000.
   b. $ 6,250.
   c. $ 4,000.
   d. $10,250.
   e. some amount other than those given.

   The correct answer is b. (CMA December 1985, 5-12)

Solution

Annual demand	5,000	units
Runs for the year	÷ 4	
Maximum inventory	1,250	units
	÷ 2	
Average inventory	625	units
Carrying cost per unit	X $ 10	
Estimated total carrying costs	$ 6,250	

4. The estimated total setup costs for the miniature oak files for the coming year is:

a. $ 5,000.
b. $ 6,250.
c. $ 4,000.
d. $10,250.
e. some amount other than those given.

The correct answer is c. (CMA December 1985, 5-13)

Solution

Setup cost per run	$ 1,000	
Runs for the year	X 4	
Estimated total setup costs	$ 4,000	

5. The number of production runs per year of the miniature oak files that would minimize the sum of carrying costs and setup costs for the coming year is:
a. 7.
b. 2.
c. 4.
d. 5.
e. some amount other than those given.

The correct answer is d. (CMA December 1985, 5-15)

Solution

$$EPR = \sqrt{\frac{2 \times 5{,}000 \times \$1{,}000}{\$10}}$$

$$= \sqrt{1{,}000{,}000}$$

$$= \underline{1{,}000}$$

Annual demand	5,000	units
Economic production run ÷	1,000	units
Production runs per year	5	

6. In production management, product breakdown into component parts and lead times for procuring these parts is necessary for:
   a. a critical path method (CPM) system.
   b. a materials requirements planning (MRP) system.
   c. a job balancing system.
   d. an economic order quantity (EOQ) system.
   e. an ABC system.

   The correct answer is b. (CMA December 1986, 5-10)

7. The inventory model that follows the concept that 80% of the value of an inventory is in 20% of the inventory items is the:
   a. ABC system.
   b. economic order quantity (EOQ) model.
   c. just-in-time inventory system.
   d. materials requirements planning (MRP) system.
   e. zero inventory model.

   The correct answer is a. (CMA December 1986, 5-11)

8. The elapsed time between placing an order for inventory and receiving the order is known as:
   a. safety-level time.
   b. lead time.
   c. reorder time.
   d. stockout time.
   e. stocking time.

   The correct answer is b. (CMA June 1988, 5-21)

9. When the level of safety stock is increased:
   a. lead time will increase.
   b. lead time will decrease.
   c. the frequency of stockouts will decrease.
   d. carrying costs will decrease.
   e. order costs will decrease.

   The correct answer is c. (CMA June 1988, 5-23)

CAPITAL ASSET SELECTION AND CAPITAL BUDGETING

Learning Objectives

After reading and studying Chapter 14, you should be able to:

1. Understand how managers choose capital budgeting projects.

2. Recognize why most capital budgeting methods use cash flows.

3. Differentiate among payback period, the net present value method, profitability index, and internal rate of return.

4. Show how taxes and depreciation methods affect cash flows.

5. Understand how the underlying assumptions and limitations of each capital project evaluation method affect their use.

6. Explain why decisions to automate are more difficult to evaluate than other capital projects.

7. Understand how and why management should conduct a post-investment audit of a capital project.

8. (Appendix 1) Use the time value of money concept.

9. (Appendix 2) Determine the accounting rate of return for a project.

Terminology

Accounting rate of return (ARR) The rate of accounting earnings obtained on the average capital investment over a project's life (from **appendix 2**)

Annuity A series of equal cash flows occurring at equal time intervals

Annuity due An annuity in which the cash flows occur at the beginning of the periods (from **appendix 1**)

Capital asset An asset used to generate revenues or cost savings by providing production, distribution, or service capabilities for more than one year

Capital budgeting A process for evaluating proposed long-range projects or courses of future activity for the purpose of allocating limited resources to desirable projects

Cash flow The receipt or disbursement of cash

Compound interest Interest calculated on the basis of principal plus interest already earned (from **appendix 1**)

Compounding period The time from one interest computation to the next (from **appendix 1**)

Cost of capital (COC) The weighted average rate that reflects the costs of the various sources of funds making up a firm's debt and equity structure

Discount rate The rate of return on capital investments required by the company; the rate of return used in present value computations

Discounting the process of removing the portion of the future cash flows that represents interest, thereby reducing those flows to present value amounts

Financing decision A judgment regarding how funds will be procured to make an acquisition

Future value (FV) The amount to which one or more sums of money invested at a specified rate will grow over a specified number of time periods (from **appendix 1**)

Hurdle rate The rate of return deemed by management to be the lowest acceptable return on investment

Independent project An investment project that has no specific bearing on any other investment project

Internal rate of return (IRR) The discount rate at which the present value of the cash inflows minus the present value of the cash outflows equals zero

Investing decision A judgment about which assets an entity will acquire to achieve its stated objectives

Mutually exclusive projects A set of proposed projects for which there is a group of available candidates that all perform essentially the same function or meet the same objective; from this group, one is chosen and all others are rejected

Mutually inclusive projects A set of proposed investments that are all related to a primary project; when the primary project is chosen, all related projects are also selected

Net present value (NPV) The difference between the present values of all the cash inflows and cash outflows of an investment project

Net present value method An investment evaluation technique that uses discounted cash flows to determine if the rate of return on a project is equal to, higher than, or lower than the desired rate of return

Ordinary annuity An annuity in which the first cash flow occurs at the end of the first period (from **appendix 1**)

Payback period The time required to recoup the original investment through cash flows from a project

Post-investment audit A procedure in which management compares actual project results against the results expected at the inception of the project

Preference decision A choice in which projects are ranked according to their impact on the achievement of company objectives

Present value (PV) The amount that a future cash flow is worth currently, given a specified rate of interest

Profitability index (PI) A ratio that compares the present value of net cash inflows with the present value of the net investment

Project A course of future investment activity; typically includes the purchase, installation, and operation of a capital asset

Rent Each equal cash flow of an annuity (from **appendix 1**)

Return of capital Recovery of the original investment

Return on capital Income; equal the discount rate times the investment amount

Screening decision A choice that indicates whether a capital project is desirable based on some previously established minimum criterion or criteria

Simple interest Interest calculated as a percentage of the original investment, or principal amount, only (from **appendix 1**)

Tax benefit (of depreciation) The depreciation provided by a capital investment multiplied by the tax rate

Tax shield (of depreciation) The amount of the reduction of taxable income provided by depreciation expense

Timeline A visual tool that illustrates the timing of expected cash receipts and payments; used for analyzing cash flows of a capital investment proposal

Lecture Outline

A. **The Investment Decision**

1. A **capital asset** is an asset used to generate revenues or cost savings by providing production, distribution, or service capabilities for more than one year.

2. **Capital budgeting** is a process for evaluating proposed long-range projects or courses of future activity for an economic entity for the purpose of allocating limited resources to desirable projects.

3. A **project** is a course of future investment activity that will typically include the purchase, installation, and operation of a capital asset.

   a. A manager's job is to make the best possible investment choices of projects and assets.

   b. Management must identify the best asset(s) for the firm to acquire in order to fulfill company goals and objectives.

4. The following four basic questions must be answered.

   a. **Is the activity worth an investment?** A company acquires assets when they have value in relation to specific activities in which the company is engaged, and the worth of an activity is initially measured by monetary cost/benefit analysis.

   b. **Which assets can be used for the activity?** The determination of the available and suitable assets for conducting the intended activity is closely related to the consideration of an activity's worth.

   c. **Of the available assets for each activity, which is the best investment?** Management should select the best asset from the candidates and exclude all others from consideration in **screening decisions** and **preference decisions**.

   d. **Of the "best investments" for all worthwhile activities, in which ones should the company invest?** Each company has a limited quantity of resources to invest at any given point in time.

5. A **screening decision** is a choice that indicates whether a capital project is desirable based on some previously established minimum criterion or criteria.

6. A **preference decision** is a choice in which projects are ranked according to their impact on the achievement of company objectives.

7. **Mutually exclusive projects** are a set of proposed projects for which there is a group of available candidates that all perform essentially the same function or meet the same objective; from this group, one is chosen and all others are rejected.

8. **Independent projects** are investment projects that have no specific bearing on any other investment projects.

9. **Mutually inclusive projects** are a set of proposed investments that are all related to a primary project; when the primary project is chosen, all related projects are also selected.

B. Cash Flows

1. **Cash flows** are the receipts or disbursements of cash.

2. Cash flows arise from the purchase, operation, and disposition of capital assets.

   a. Cash receipts include project revenues that have been earned and collected, savings generated by reduced project operating costs, and inflows from the asset's sale and/or release of working capital at the end of the asset's useful life.

   b. Cash disbursements include expenditures to acquire the asset, additional working capital investments, and amounts paid for related operating costs.

3. Interest is a cash flow caused by the financing method used for the project and is not a factor that should be considered in project evaluation.

   a. A **financing decision** is a judgment regarding the method of procuring funds that will be used to make an acquisition.

   b. An **investing decision** is a judgment about which assets will be acquired by an entity to achieve its stated objectives.

4. Cash flows from a capital project are received and paid at different times during a project's life.

   a. Some cash flows occur at the beginning of a period, other cash flows occur during the period, while others occur at the end.

   b. Analysts assume that the occurrence of cash flows always occurs at either the beginning or the end of the time period during which they actually occur in order to simplify capital budgeting analysis.

   c. Cash flows assumed to occur at the end of the period include inflows provided by product sales' contribution margin and outflows for repair expenditures and property taxes on the capital asset.

5. A **return of capital** is simply recovery of the original investment.

6. **Return on capital** represents income; equals the discount rate times the investment amount.

7. A **timeline** is a visual tool that illustrates the timing of expected cash receipts and payments; used for analyzing cash flows of a capital investment proposal.

8. An **annuity** is a series of equal cash flows occurring at equal time intervals.

C. **Payback Period**

1. A project's **payback period** is the time required to recoup the original investment through cash flows from a project.

   a. The payback period is determined as follows when the cash flow of a project is a simple annuity:

      Payback Period = Investment Cost ÷ Projected Annuity Inflow Amount

   b. The underlying assumption of the payback period is that the longer it takes to recover the initial investment, the greater the project's risk.

   c. The payback period for a project having unequal cash inflows is determined by accumulating cash flows until the original investment is recovered.

2. Company management often sets a maximum acceptable payback period as part of its evaluation techniques for capital projects.

3. The payback period method ignores three important aspects: (1) inflows occurring after the payback period has been reached, (2) the company's desired rate of return, and (3) the time value of money.

D. Discounted Cash Flow Methods

1. **Discounting** is the process of removing the portion of the future cash flows that represents interest, thereby reducing those flows to present value amounts.

2. A project's **net present value (NPV)** is the difference between the present values of all the cash inflows and cash outflows of an investment project.

3. The **discount rate** is the rate of return on capital investments required by the company; the rate of return used in present value computations.

4. The **cost of capital (COC)** is the weighted average rate that reflects the costs of the various sources of funds making up a firm's debt and equity structure.

5. The **net present value method** is an investment evaluation technique that uses discounted cash flows to determine if the rate of return on a project is equal to, higher than, or lower than the desired rate of return.

   a. The actual rate of return on the project is equal to the desired rate of return if the NPV is zero.

   b. The actual rate of return on the project is greater than the desired rate of return if the NPV is positive.

   c. The actual rate of return on the project is less than the desired rate of return if the NPV is negative.

   d. The net present value method provides information on how the actual rate compares to the desired rate, allowing managers to eliminate from consideration any projects on which the rates of return are less than the desired rate and, therefore, not acceptable.

6. The **profitability index (PI)** is a ratio that compares the present value of net cash inflows to the present value of the net investment.

$$PI = \frac{\text{Present Value of Net Future Cash Flows}}{\text{Present Value of Investment}}$$

   a. The present value of the net cash inflows represents an output measure of the project's worth, and is equal to the cash benefit provided by the project or the present value of future cash inflows minus the present value of future cash outflows.

   b. The present value of the investment represents an input measure of the project's cost.

   c. The profitability index gauges the firm's efficiency of utilizing capital; the higher the index, the more efficient are the firm's investments.

   d. Two conditions must exist for the PI to provide better information than the NPV method: ① the projects must be mutually exclusive and ② there must be limited availability of investment funds.

   e. A firm that makes capital budgeting decisions on a profitability basis would judge a project as acceptable if the project's PI is equal to or greater than 1.00.

7. The **internal rate of return (IRR)** is the discount rate at which the present value of the cash inflows minus the present value of the cash outflows equals zero; it is a project's expected rate of return.

   a. The IRR is determined by calculating a factor that can then be matched with a factor in the present value of an ordinary annuity of $1 table for projects having equal annual net cash flows.

   b. The IRR for a project that does not have equal annual net cash flows requires an iterative trial and error process.

   c. A company's **hurdle rate** is the rate of return deemed by management to be the lowest acceptable return on investment, and a project is considered to be a viable investment if its IRR is equal to or greater than the hurdle rate.

E. **Assumptions and Limitations of Methods** (see text **Exhibit 14-8**)

1. Managers should understand the basic similarities and differences of the various methods and use several techniques to evaluate a project.

2. All methods have two identical limitations: (1) they do not consider management preferences about the timing of cash flows and (2) they use a single, deterministic measure of cash flow amounts rather than ranges of cash flow values based on probabilities.

3. The first limitation can be compensated for by subjectively favoring projects whose cash flow profiles better suit management's preferences, assuming other project factors are equal; and the second limitation can be overcome by using probability estimates of cash flows.

F. **The Effect of Taxation on Cash Flows**

1. Managers should give complete recognition to income tax implications of all company decisions and should use after-tax cash flows to determine project acceptability in evaluating capital projects.

2. Depreciation of capital assets is deductible in computing taxable income.

   a. A **tax shield (of depreciation)** is the amount of the reduction of taxable income provided by depreciation expense.

   b. A **tax benefit (of depreciation)** is the depreciation provided by a capital investment multiplied by the tax rate.

3. Managers need to use the most current depreciation regulations to calculate cash flows from projects.

4. Capital projects are analyzed and evaluated before investments are made and managers should be aware of the inherent risk of changes in tax law or in the tax rate structure.

G. **Illustration of After-Tax Cash Flows in Capital Budgeting** (see text **Exhibit 14-10**)

H. **High-Tech Investments**

1. Purchases of automated and robotic equipment are some of the most important investment decisions American companies have to make.

   a. High-technology equipment usually requires massive investments, and significant thought should be given to the tangible and intangible benefits generated by such investments.

   b. Management must consider the interdependent relationships of such investments, including significantly reduced labor costs, increased quality and quantity of production, shortened processing time, and increased utility and maintenance costs.

2. Outlays for factory automation are expected to increase substantially during the 1990s, and the rationale for the slowness by companies to invest in automated equipment is multifaceted.

   a. One reason has been a desire to minimize worker displacement and the corresponding increase in unemployment; a basic robot can do the work of up to six employees depending on the tasks involved.

   b. A second concern has been morale problems of employees who retain their jobs after some degree of automation has occurred; such employees often feel guilty because they kept their jobs and uneasy about having to learn new skills.

   c. Management has found that automated equipment often does not work correctly, is difficult to integrate with non-automated equipment, or does not do as good a job as had been done by humans.

3. Traditional capital budgeting analysis may need some modifications to be more useful to managers making automated equipment investment decisions, and four modifications to the analysis process are suggested.

   a. Managers need to be more careful in setting the discount rate used to determine present value figures.

   b. More weight needs to be given to the qualitative benefits to be provided by the capital expenditure.

   c. High-tech investment projects are not "free-standing," and such investments should be considered as interrelated elements of an integrated strategy rather than as individual projects.

d. Consideration should be given to the opportunity cost of *not* acquiring automated equipment.

4. Managers, in making capital budgeting decisions, should quantify all benefits and costs that can be quantified with any reasonable degree of accuracy.

   a. Such quantifications are extremely necessary when evaluating high-technology equipment expenditures.

   b. Managers can attempt to quantify the *qualitative* benefits using probabilities and recalculate the investment's net present value and/or IRR to check for financial acceptability. (see text **Exhibit 14-11**)

I. **Illustration of High-Tech Investment Analysis** (see text **Exhibit 14-12**)

J. **Post-Investment Audit**

1. A **post-investment audit** is a procedure in which management compares actual project results against the results expected at the inception of the project.

2. The post-investment audit process is intended to accomplish at least four primary objectives: (1) serve as an important financial control mechanism, (2) provide information for future capital expenditure decisions, (3) remove certain psychological and/or political impediments usually associated with asset control and abandonment, and (4) have a psychological impact on those proposing capital investments.

3. Post-investment audits become more crucial as the size of capital expenditures increase.

   a. A post-investment audit can be used to pinpoint areas of operations that are not in line with expectations for the purpose of correcting problems before they get out of hand.

   b. Management should take action to find the causes of any adverse differences and the means, if possible, to remedy them.

4. The performance of a post-investment audit is difficult for several reasons.

    a. Actual information may be found in a different form than the original estimates, and some project benefits may be difficult to quantify.

    b. Project returns vary considerably over time, so that results gathered at a given point in time may not be representative of the project.

5. Post-investment audits provide management with information that can help to make better capital investment decisions in the future.

K. Time Value of Money – Appendix 1

1. **Future value (FV)** refers to the amount to which one or more sums of money invested at a specified interest rate will grow over a specified number of time periods.

2. **Present value** is the amount that a future cash flow is worth currently, given a specified rate of interest.

3. Future and present values depend on three things: (1) amount of the cash flow, (2) rate of interest, and (3) timing of the cash flow.

4. **Simple interest** is interest that is calculated as a percentage of the original investment, or principal amount, only.

5. **Compound interest** is interest that is calculated on the basis of principal plus interest already earned.

6. The **compounding period** is the time from one interest computation to the next.

7. A present value of a single cash flow is simply a future value discounted back the same number of periods at the same rate of interest as it would require to compound from the resulting present value to the same future value.

8. The **discount rate** is the rate of return on capital investments required by the company; the rate of return used in present value computations.

9. An **annuity** is a series of equal cash flows occurring at equal time intervals.

   a. An **ordinary annuity** is an annuity in which the first cash flow occurs at the end of the first period.

   b. An **annuity due** is an annuity in which the cash flows occur at the beginning of the periods.

   c. A **rent** is each equal cash flow of an annuity.

L. **Accounting Rate of Return**

   1. The **accounting rate of return (ARR)** is the rate of accounting earnings obtained on the average capital investment over a project's life.

   $$ARR = \frac{\text{Average Annual Profits from Project}}{\text{Average Investment in Project}}$$

   2. Project investment includes original cost and project support costs, such as those needed for working capital items.

   3. Investment, salvage value, and working capital released at the end of the project's life are summed and divided by two to obtain the **average investment**.

   4. A project's calculated ARR is compared with a preestablished ARR hurdle rate set by management which may be higher than the discount rate since the method does not include the time value of money.

Multiple Choice Questions from CMA Examinations

1. Depreciation is incorporated explicitly in the discounted cash flow analysis of an investment proposal because it:
   a. is a cost of operations that cannot be avoided.
   b. results in an annual cash outflow.
   c. is a cash inflow.
   d. reduces the cash outlay for income taxes.
   e. represents the initial cash outflow spread over the life of the investment.

   The correct answer is d. (CMA December 1977, 5-14)

2. Future, Inc. is in the enviable situation of having unlimited capital funds. The best decision rule, in an economic sense, for it to follow would be to invest in all projects in which the:
   a. payback is less than four years.
   b. accounting rate of return is greater than the earnings as a percent of sales.
   c. payback reciprocal is greater than the internal rate of return.
   d. the internal rate of return is greater than zero.
   e. net present value is greater than zero.

   The correct answer is e. (CMA December 1978, 5-12)

Questions 3 through 6 are based on the following information. Yipann Corporation is reviewing an investment proposal. The initial cost as well as other related data for each year are presented in the schedule below. All cash flows are assumed to take place at the end of the year. The salvage value of the investment at the end each year is equal to its net book value, and there will be no salvage value at the end of the investment's life.

Investment Proposal

Year	Initial Cost and Book Value	Annual Net After-Tax Cash Flows	Annual Net Income
0	$ 105,000	$ -0-	$ -0-
1	70,000	50,000	15,000
2	42,000	45,000	17,000
3	21,000	40,000	19,000
4	7,000	35,000	21,000
5	-0-	30,000	23,000

Yipann uses a 24% after-tax target rate of return for new investment proposals. The discount figures for a 24% rate of return are given below.

Year	Present Value of $1.00 Received at the End of Period	Present Value of an Annuity of $1.00 Received at the End of Each Period
1	.81	.81
2	.65	1.46
3	.52	1.98
4	.42	2.40
5	.34	2.74
6	.28	3.02
7	.22	3.24

3. The traditional payback period for the investment proposal is:
   a. 0.875 years.
   b. 1.933 years.
   c. 2.250 years.
   d. over 5 years.
   e. some period other than those given above.

   The correct answer is c. (CMA December 1991, 4-1)

Solution

	Investment		
Year	Recovered Through Cash Flows	Unrecovered	Years
0		$ 105,000	
1	$ 50,000	55,000	1.00
2	45,000	10,000	1.00
3	10,000	-0-	.25 ($10,000 ÷ $40,000)
			2.25

4. The average annual cash inflow at which Yipann would be indifferent to the investment (rounded to the nearest dollar) is:
   a. $21,000.
   b. $30,000.
   c. $38,321.
   d. $46,667.
   e. $50,000.

   The correct answer is c. (CMA December 1991, 4-2)

Solution

$$\$105,000 \div 2.74 = \$38,321$$

5. The accounting rate of return for the investment proposal over its life using the initial value of the investment is:
   a. 36.2%.
   b. 18.1%.
   c. 28.1%.
   d. 38.1%.
   e. 24.0%.

The correct answer is b. (CMA December 1991, 4-3)

Solution

Year	Net Income	
1	$ 15,000	
2	17,000	
3	19,000	
4	21,000	
5	23,000	
	$ 95,000	Total Net Income
÷	5	Years
	$ 19,000	Average Net Income
÷	$ 105,000	Initial Investment
	18.1%	ARR

6. The net present value of the investment proposal is:
   a. $ 4,600 .
   b. $ 10,450 .
   c. $<55,250>.
   d. $115,450 .
   e. $105,000 .

The correct answer is b. (CMA December 1991, 4-4)

Solution

Year	Annual Net After-Tax Cash Flows	Present Value of $1 Factor	Present Value of Cash Flows	
1	$ 50,000	.81	$ 40,500	
2	45,000	.65	29,250	
3	40,000	.52	20,800	
4	35,000	.42	14,700	
5	30,000	.34	10,200	
			$ 115,450	Total Present Value
			<105,000>	Investment
			$ 10,450	Net Present Value

RESPONSIBILITY ACCOUNTING AND TRANSFER PRICING IN DECENTRALIZED OPERATIONS

Learning Objectives

After reading and studying Chapter 15, you should be able to:

1. Discuss when decentralized operations are appropriate.

2. Relate responsibility accounting to decentralization.

3. Differentiate among the four types of responsibility centers.

4. Discuss the concept and effects of suboptimization.

5. Differentiate among various definitions of product cost.

6. Understand how and why transfer prices for services are used internally in organizations.

7. Understand how and why transfer prices for services are used internally in organizations.

Terminology

Centralization An organizational structure in which top management makes most decisions and controls most activities of the organizational units from the company's central headquarters

Cost center An organizational unit in which the manager has the authority only to incur costs and is specifically evaluated on the basis of how well costs are controlled

Critical success factor An item that is so important to an organization that, without it, the organization would fail; quality, customer service, efficiency, cost control, and responsiveness to change are five basic critical success factors

Decentralization An organizational structure in which top management grants subordinate managers a significant degree of autonomy and independence in operating and making decisions for their organizational units

Dual pricing arrangement A transfer price method that allows a selling division to record the transfer of goods or services at a market-based or negotiated price and a buying division to record the transfer at a cost-based amount

Goal congruence A condition that exists when the personal and organizational goals of decision makers throughout a firm are consistent and mutually supportive

Investment center An organizational unit in which the manager is responsible for generating revenues, planning and controlling costs, and acquiring, disposing of, and using plant assets to earn the highest feasible rate of return on the investment base

Negotiated transfer price An intracompany charge for goods or services that has been set through a process of negotiation between the selling and purchasing unit managers

Profit center An organizational unit in which the manager is responsible for generating revenues and planning and controlling all expenses

Responsibility accounting An accounting system that provides information to top management about segment or subunit performance

Responsibility center The cost object under the control of a manager; in the case of a decentralized company, the cost object is an organizational unit such as a division, department, or geographical region

Responsibility report A report that reflects the revenues and/or costs under the control of a specific unit manager

Revenue center An organizational unit in which the manager is accountable only for the generation of revenues and has no control over setting selling prices or budgeting costs

Suboptimization A situation in which unit managers make decisions that positively affect their own unit, but are detrimental to other organizational units or to the company as a whole

Transfer price An internal charge established for the exchange of goods or services between organizational units of the same company

Lecture Outline

A. **Decentralization**

1. The extent to which authority is retained by top management (**centralization**) or released from top management and passed to lower managerial levels (**decentralization**) can be viewed as a continuum, and either end of the continuum represents a clearly undesirable arrangement. (see text **Exhibit 15-1**)

2. **Centralization** is an organizational structure in which top management makes most decisions and controls most activities of the organizational units from the company's central headquarters.

    a. A single individual (normally the company owner or president) performs all decision making and retains full authority and responsibility for that organization's activities in a totally centralized firm.

    b. The single individual may not have the expertise or sufficient and timely information to make decisions in all areas.

3. **Decentralization** is an organizational strategy in which top management grants subordinate managers a significant degree of autonomy and independence in operating and making decisions for their organizational units.

    a. A purely decentralized organization has virtually no central authority and each subunit acts as a totally independent entity.

    b. Subunits may act in ways that are not consistent with the goals of the total organization.

4. The extent of decentralization in an organization may not be quantifiable.

5. Decentralization depends on the type of organizational units that are in a firm.

6. Top management must consider the subunit managers' personalities and perceived abilities.

   a. Managers in decentralized environments must be goal-oriented, assertive, decisive, and creative.

   b. Such managers must also be willing to accept the authority delegated by top management and to be judged on the outcomes of the decisions that they make.

7. Decentralization does not necessarily mean that a unit manager has the authority to make all decisions concerning that unit.

8. Top management selectively determines the types of authority to delegate and the types to withhold.

9. Decentralization has many personnel advantages.

   a. Managers have the need and occasion to develop their leadership skills, and decentralized units provide excellent settings for training personnel and for screening aspiring managers for promotion.

   b. Managers can be judged on job performance and on the results of their units as compared to units headed by other managers; such comparisons usually encourage a healthy level of organizational competition.

   c. Decentralization often leads to greater job satisfaction for managers since it provides for job enrichment and gives a feeling of increased importance to the organization.

   d. The manager of a decentralized unit has more knowledge of the local operating environment, which results in the following: ① reduction in the time it takes to make decisions, ② minimization of difficulties that may result from attempting to communicate problems and instructions through an organizational chain of command, and ③ quicker perceptions of environmental changes than is possible for top management.

   e. A decentralized structure allows the management by exception principle to be implemented.

10. Decentralization also has is disadvantages.

   a. Decision-making authority may be divided among too many
      individuals.

   b. Unit managers in a decentralized company compete with one another
      since the results of unit activities are compared; they therefore may
      make decisions that positively affect their own units, but are detrimental
      to other organizational units or to the overall organization. Such
      suboptimization may be prevented or overcome by encouraging goal
      congruence. **Goal congruence** exists when the personal and
      organizational goals of decision makers throughout a firm are consistent
      and mutually supportive.

   c. A decentralized organization requires that more effective methods of
      communicating plans, activities, and achievements be established since
      decision making is removed from the central office, so that top
      management must be constantly cognizant of events occurring at lower
      levels in order to determine if operations are progressing toward
      established goals.

   d. Decentralization may be extremely costly; a duplication of activities can
      be created that could be quite expensive in terms of both time and
      money.

B. **Responsibility Accounting Systems**

1. **Responsibility accounting** refers to an accounting system that provides
   information to top management about segment or subunit performance.

2. **Responsibility reports** are reports that reflect the revenues and/or costs
   under the control of a specific unit manager.

   a. The number of responsibility reports issued at a specific point in time for
      a decentralized unit depends on the degree of influence its manager has
      on the unit's day-to-day operations and costs, so that a manager's strong
      influence will result in one report being sufficient for both the manager
      and the unit.

b. Some unit costs are not normally controlled (or are only partially or indirectly controlled) by the unit manager, causing the responsibility report to take one of two forms: ① a single report can be issued that shows all costs incurred in the unit, separately classified as either controllable or noncontrollable by the manager, or ② separate reports can be prepared for the unit manager and the organizational unit.

3. A responsibility accounting system is an important tool in making decentralization work effectively.

a. The responsibility reports relating to unit performance are mainly designed to fit the planning, controlling, and decision making needs of subordinate managers.

b. Top managers review the reports in order to evaluate the efficiency and effectiveness of each unit and each manager.

4. One purpose of a responsibility accounting system is to "secure control at the point where costs are incurred instead of assigning them all to products and processes remote from the point of incurrence," which is in agreement with the concepts of standard costing and activity-based costing.

5. Control procedures are implemented for the following three reasons:

a. Managers attempt to cause actual operating results to conform to planned results, and such conformity is known as effectiveness.

b. Managers attempt to cause, at a minimum, the standard output to be produced from the actual input costs incurred, and such conformity is known as efficiency.

c. Managers need to ensure, to the extent possible, a reasonable utilization of plant and equipment.

6. Responsibility accounting implies acceptance of communicated authority from top management by subordinate managers.

a. The responsibility accounting system is designed so that actual data are captured in conformity with budgetary accounts.

b. Operating reports comparing actual and budgetary account balances are prepared periodically and issued to managers.

c. Managers should have: ① been aware of significant variances before they were reported, ② identified variance causes, and ③ attempted to correct causes of problems.

d. Top management may not know about operational variances until responsibility reports are received, at which time the problems causing the variances should have been corrected or subordinate managers should have explanations as to why the problems were not or could not have been resolved.

e. The flexible budget may be a more appropriate basis for a responsibility report than a static budget.

7. The performance reports of each layer of management are reviewed and evaluated by each successive management layer, so that responsibility reports can motivate managers to influence operations in ways that will reflect positive performance.

8. A **responsibility center** is the cost object under the control of a manager; in the case of a decentralized company, the cost object is an organizational unit such as a division, department, or geographical region.

C. Types of Responsibility Centers

1. A **cost center** is an organizational unit in which the manager only has the authority to incur costs and is specifically evaluated on the basis of how well costs are controlled.

   a. Revenues do not exist in many cost centers since the organizational unit does not engage in any revenue-producing activity.

   b. Revenues, in other instances, may exist for a particular subunit but they are either not under the manager's control or are not effectively measurable.

   c. A standard costing system is traditionally used and variances are reported and analyzed, with top management often concentrating only on the unfavorable variances occurring in a cost center and ignoring the efficient performance indicated by favorable variances.

   d. Top management, using the management by exception principle, should investigate all favorable and unfavorable variances that fall outside the range of acceptable deviations.

2. A **revenue center** is an organizational unit in which the manager is accountable only for the generation of revenues and has no control over setting selling prices or budgeting costs.

   a. Managers of "revenue centers" are usually responsible not only for revenues, but are also involved in the planning and control over at least some of the costs incurred in the center.

   b. Salaries that are directly traceable to the center are often a cost responsibility of the "revenue center" manager, reflecting the traditional retail environment in which a sales clerk was assigned to a specific department and was only allowed to check out customers wanting to purchase the department's merchandise.

3. A **profit center** is an organizational unit in which the manager is responsible for generating revenues and planning and controlling all expenses.

   a. The major goal of a profit center manager is to maximize the center's net income.

   b. Profit centers should be independent organizational units so that the managers have the ability to obtain resources at the most economical prices and to sell products at prices that will maximize revenue.

4. An **investment center** is an organizational unit in which the manager is responsible for generating revenues, planning and controlling costs, and acquiring, disposing of, and using plant assets to earn the highest feasible rate of return on the investment base.

   a. Many investment centers are independent, free-standing divisions or subsidiaries of a firm, allowing the center managers the opportunity to make decisions about all matters affecting their organizational units and to be judged on the outcomes of those decisions.

   b. Managers of responsibility centers are encouraged, to the extent possible, to operate such centers as separate economic entities that exist for the same basic organizational goal if those centers are designated as profit and investment centers.

D. Suboptimization

1. **Critical success factors** are those items that are so important to an organization that, without them, the organization would fail; quality, customer service, efficiency, cost control, and responsiveness to change are five basic critical success factors.

2. **Suboptimization** exists when unit managers make decisions that positively affect their own unit, but are detrimental to other organizational units or to the company as a whole.

3. Top management must be aware of suboptimization and must develop methods to avoid it in order for it to be limited or minimized.

E. Transfer Pricing (see text Exhibit 15-11)

1. A **transfer price** is an internal charge established for the exchange of goods or services between organizational units of the same company.

   a. Transfer prices are often used for internal reporting purposes in a company that has independent segments or divisions.

   b. Internal company transfers should be presented at the producing segment's costs for external reporting purposes; so that if transfers are "sold" at an amount other than cost, any intersegment profit, expense, and/or revenue accounts must be eliminated.

2. The general rules for choosing a transfer price are:

   a. The maximum price should be no greater than the lowest market price at which the buying segment can acquire the goods or services externally.

   b. The minimum price should be no less than the sum of the selling segment's incremental production costs plus the opportunity cost of the facilities used. (Incremental cost refers to the additional cost of producing a contemplated quantity of output; this amount generally reflects variable costs of production.)

   c. Any transfer price set between the two limits is usually considered appropriate.

3. The transfer price is equal to total unit absorption cost or variable cost when **cost-based transfer prices** are used.

4. Some companies use **market-based transfer prices** to eliminate the problems of defining *cost*; market price is believed to be an objective measure of value and simulates the selling price that would exist if the segments were independent companies.

5. **Negotiated transfer prices** constitute intracompany charges for goods or services that have been set through a process of negotiation between the selling and purchasing unit managers.

6. **Dual pricing arrangements** include methods of transfer pricing that allow a selling division to record transfers of goods or services at market-based or negotiated prices and a buying division to record transfers at cost-based amounts.

7. The final determination of what transfer pricing system to use should reflect the circumstances of the organizational units and corporate goals; no one method of setting a transfer price is best in all instances.

8. Transfer prices are not permanent; they are frequently revised in reaction to changes in costs, supply, demand, competitive forces, and other factors.

9. A thoughtfully set transfer price, regardless of the method used, will provide the following advantages: (1) an appropriate basis for the calculation and evaluation of segment performance, (2) the rational acquisition or use of goods and services between corporate divisions, (3) the flexibility to respond to changes in demand or market conditions, and (4) a means of motivating managers in decentralized operations.

F. **Transfer Prices for Service Departments**

1. Transfer price applications for services are commonly found in governmental and not-for-profit organizations.

2. A department, in setting a transfer price for services, must decide on a capacity level to use in price development. (see text **Exhibit 15-13**)

3. The transfer price per unit of service will be higher if expected capacity is chosen than it would if practical capacity were chosen.

4. General costs need to be allocated to the various departments equitably in developing transfer prices for services, and in determining the underlying reason for cost incurrence.

G. **Transfer Pricing in Multinational Settings** (see text **Exhibit 15-15**)

1. The setting of transfer prices for products and services becomes quite
    difficult when the company is engaged in multinational operations due to
    differences in tax systems, customs duties, freight and insurance costs,
    import/export regulations, and foreign exchange controls.

2. **Multinational enterprises (MNEs)** have transfer pricing policies with
    internal and external objectives that differ, so there is no simple answer to
    setting transfer prices.

3. Some guidelines as to transfer pricing policies among countries should be
    set by the company and followed on a consistent basis.

4. Multinational companies can determine the effectiveness of their transfer
    pricing policies by using two criteria: (1) does the system achieve
    economic decisions that positively affect MNE performance, including
    international capital investment decisions, output level decisions for both
    intermediate and final products, and product pricing decisions for external
    customers? and (2) do subsidiary managers believe that they are being
    fairly evaluated and rewarded for their divisional contributions to the
    MNE as a whole?

5. The company, if the answer to both of the previous two questions [4. (1) and
    (2)] is yes, would appear to have a transfer pricing system that
    appropriately coordinates the underlying considerations, minimizes the
    internal and external goal conflicts, and balances short-range and long-
    range perspectives of the MNE.

Multiple Choice Questions from CMA Examinations

1. The Hersh Company uses a performance reporting system that reflects the company's decentralization of decision making. The departmental performance report shows one line of data for each subordinate who reports to the group vice president. The data presented show the actual costs incurred during the period, the budgeted costs, and all variances from budget for that subordinate's department. The Hersh Company is using a type of system called:
   a. contribution accounting.
   b. cost-benefit accounting.
   c. flexible budgeting.
   d. program budgeting.
   e. responsibility accounting.

   The correct answer is e. (CMA June 1989, 4-25)

MEASURING AND REWARDING PERFORMANCE

Learning Objectives

After reading and studying Chapter 16, you should be able to:

1. Discuss the need for multiple performance measures.

2. Compare and contrast return on investment and residual income.

3. Explain why nonfinancial measures are important to evaluating performance.

4. Identify some reasons why it is more difficult to measure performance in multinational firms than in solely domestic companies.

5. Discuss how employee rewards (including compensation) and performance should be related.

6. Explain how expatriate reward systems may differ from those of domestic operations.

Terminology

Asset turnover A ratio that measures asset productivity and shows the number of sales dollars generated by each dollar of assets

Compensation strategy A foundation for the compensation plan that addresses the role compensation should play in the organization

Du Pont model A model that indicates the return on investment as it is affected by profit margin and asset turnover

Expatriate A parent company or third-country national assigned to a foreign subsidiary or a foreign national assigned to the parent company

Process productivity Total units produced during a period using value-added processing time

Process quality yield The proportion of good units that resulted from the activities expended

Profit margin The ratio of income to sales

Residual income (RI) Profit earned that exceeds an amount "charged" for funds committed to a responsibility center

Return on investment (ROI) A ratio that relates income generated by the investment center to the resources (or asset base) used to produce that income

Synchronous management All endeavors that help an organization achieve its goals

Lecture Outline

A. **Measuring Organizational and Employee Performance**

1. Four general rules relating to performance measurement should be established.

   a. Measures should be established that assess progress toward organizational goals and objectives.

   b. Persons being evaluated should be aware of the measurements to be used and have had some input in developing them.

   c. Persons being evaluated should have the appropriate skills, equipment, information, and authority to be successful under the measurement system.

   d. Feedback of accomplishment relative to performance should be provided in a timely and useful manner.

2. The first general rule establishes the reason for using multiple performance measures.

   a. A primary goal is to be financially able to continue in existence, and if the organization is profit-oriented, this goal is satisfied by generating a net income amount considered to be satisfactory relative to the assets invested.

   b. Some relevant financial performance measures are therefore necessary for the type of company or organizational unit being evaluated, and it is equally necessary that any chosen measures reflect an understanding of accounting information and its potential for being manipulated.

   c. Many companies have now established the nonfinancial organizational goals of customer satisfaction, zero defects, minimal lead time to market, and social responsibility with regard to the environment.

   d. Nonfinancial performance measures can be developed, while the organization is in business, that can indicate progress, or lack thereof, toward the achievement of the important critical success factors of a world-class company.

3. Top management must set high performance standards and communicate such standards to lower-level managers and employees, and the measures should promote harmonious operations among organizational units.

a. People will usually act in accordance with the way they are to be measured, so it is essential that the individuals be cognizant of and understand the performance measures to be used.

b. Employees will not be allowed to perform at their highest level of potential if information about measures is withheld from them, and such withholding of information will not allow for feelings of mutual respect and cooperation.

c. People are more likely to be committed to the process if they participated in setting the standards or the budget if actual-to-standard or actual-to-budget comparisons are to be used as performance measures.

4. The organization is responsible for making certain that either job skills exist or can be obtained through available training.

a. Competent people must then be given the necessary tools (equipment, information, and authority) to perform their jobs in a fashion consistent with the measurement process.

b. People cannot be expected to be able to accomplish their tasks if the appropriate tools are unavailable.

5. Managerial performance should be *monitored* (though not *evaluated*) on an ongoing basis, and feedback should be provided.

a. Positive feedback serves to motivate employees to future successes by encouraging employees to continue favorable behaviors.

b. Employees that receive negative feedback are made aware of problems and can attempt to modify behaviors.

c. Performance measurement has usually relied on information generated during the management control process.

d. This type of measurement system was easy to implement, but it often concentrated on performance attributes that were not the most conducive to sound competitive positions. Traditional performance measures are therefore being supplemented with some additional ones.

6. The traditional focus of performance measurement at the managerial level has been on financial aspects of operations and has concentrated on monetary measures such as: (1) divisional profits, (2) achievement of budget objectives, (3) individual and total variances from budget or standard, and (4) cash flow.

B. Financial Performance Measurements for Managers

1. The type of responsibility center being evaluated affects the performance measure(s) used since people should only be evaluated using performance measures relating to their authority and responsibility.

   a. The primary financial performance measure for a cost center is the materiality of the variances from budgeted costs.

   b. Performance can be judged in a pure revenue center primarily by comparing budgeted to actual revenues.

   c. Profit and investment center managers are responsible for both revenues and expenses; therefore other performance measures can be used in addition to the measures used by cost and revenue centers.

2. The **segment margin** of a profit center or the income of an investment center is frequently used as a measure of divisional performance. The term *segment margin* relates directly to the term *product margin*. (see text **Chapter 9**)

   a. The actual segment margin is compared with the center's budgeted income objective and variances are calculated to determine where objectives were exceeded or were not achieved.

   b. One problem in using the segment margin as a performance measure is that the individual components used to derive it are subject to manipulation.

   c. Divisional segment margin or income represents a short-term objective, and most reward systems (promotion, pay raises, bonuses) are based on short-term performance.

3. **Cash flow** is another valid performance measure.

   a. Management's attention may become diverted from the size and direction of cash inflows and outflows by the use of accrual-based segment margin or income as a performance measure.

   b. The **Statement of Cash Flows (SCF)** helps to correct this situation by providing information about the cash impacts of the three major categories of business activities: ① operating, ② investing, and ③ financing.

   c. The SCF explains the change in the cash balance by indicating the entity's sources and uses of cash.

   d. Cash flow can be manipulated as easily as segment margins and income, and relates to the short-run rather than the long-run.

4. **Return on investment (ROI)** is a ratio that relates income generated by the investment center to the resources (or asset base) used to produce that income. (see text **Exhibits 16-2 and 16-3**)

   a. The ROI formula is:

   $$ROI = \frac{Income}{Assets\ Invested}$$

   b. Managers of investment centers can be judged in relation to the return on investment earned by their organizational units.

   c. Both terms in the formula must be specifically defined before the ROI calculation can be used effectively as a performance measure to evaluate an investment center and to make intracompany, intercompany, and multinational comparisons.

d. The **Du Pont model** is a model that indicates the return on investment as it is affected by **profit margin** and **asset turnover**. **Profit margin** is the ratio of income to sales, and **asset turnover** is a ratio that measures asset productivity and shows the number of sales dollars generated by each dollar of assets.

ROI = Profit Margin X Asset Turnover

$$ROI = \frac{Income}{Sales} \times \frac{Sales}{Assets\ Invested}$$

e. ROI is affected by decisions involving sales prices, volume and mix of products sold, expenses, and capital asset acquisitions and dispositions.

f. ROI can possibly be increased through various management options including: ① improving profit margins by raising sales prices without impairing demand, ② decreasing expenses; and ③ decreasing dollars invested in assets, especially if those assets are no longer productive.

g. Assessments as to whether profit margin, asset turnover, and ROI are favorable or unfavorable can only be made by comparing actual results for each component with some valid basis — such as expected results, prior results, or results of other similar entities.

h. Unfavorable rates of return should be perceived as managerial opportunities for improvement, and factors used in the calculation should be analyzed for more detailed information.

5. **Residual income (RI)** is the profit earned that exceeds an amount "charged" for funds committed to a responsibility center.

   a. The RI calculation is:

   Residual Income = Income - (Target Rate X Asset Base)

   b. The advantage of RI over ROI is that RI is expressed as a dollar figure rather than as a percentage.

   c. One difficulty in using residual income as a performance measure is that it is hard to make valid comparisons among divisions of various sizes.

6. ROI and RI both have certain limitations when used to measure investment center performance.

   a. Income can be manipulated on a short-run basis.

   b. Asset investment is difficult to properly measure and assign to center managers.

   c. The use of ROI and RI may cause suboptimization of resources by concentrating attention on how well an investment center itself performs, rather than how well that center performs in relation to company-wide objectives.

C. Nonfinancial Performance Measures

1. Managerial performance can be evaluated using both qualitative and quantitative measures, and qualitative measures are often subjective.

2. Managers are usually more comfortable with and respond better to quantitative measures of performance since such measures provide a defined target at which to aim. Quantifiable performance measures are of two types: nonfinancial and financial.

3. Managers traditionally have conducted performance evaluations based almost exclusively on financial results.

4. Both financial and nonfinancial measures should be utilized in a progressively designed performance measurement system, especially those measures that track the factors essential for world-class status.

5. **Nonfinancial performance measures (NFPM)** include statistics for activities such as on-time delivery, manufacturing cycle time, setup time, defect rate, number of unplanned production interruptions, and customer returns.

6. NFPMs have two distinct advantages over financial performance measures:

   a. Nonfinancial indicators directly measure an entity's performance in the activities that create shareholder wealth, such as manufacturing and delivering quality goods and services and providing service for the customer.

   b. Nonfinancial measures may better predict the direction of future cash flows since they measure productive activity directly.

7. Management should strive to identify the firm's critical success factors and to choose a few qualitative attributes of each NFPM that managers wish to continuously improve.

   a. Nonfinancial critical success factors could include ① quality, ② customer satisfaction, ③ manufacturing efficiency and effectiveness, ④ technical excellence, and ⑤ rapid response to market demands.

   b. Management should target, for each success factor chosen, a few attributes of each relevant NFPM for continuous improvement; the attributes should include both short-run and long-run success measures to properly steer organizational activities.

8. Managers should establish acceptable performance levels to provide bases of comparison against which actual statistical data can be compared once the NFPMs have been selected. (see text **Exhibit 16-9**)

   a. Such benchmark comparison bases can be developed internally or determined from external sources.

   b. Each employee, in each area in which a performance measurement is to be made, must agree ① to accept specific responsibility for performance and ② to be evaluated.

9. **Throughput** refers to the total number of good units or quantity of services produced and sold by an organization during a time period. (see text **Chapter 13**)

   a. **Synchronous management** includes all endeavors that help an organization achieve its goals; its strategic objective is to simultaneously increase throughput while reducing inventory and operating expenses.

   b. One way to measure throughput is to view it as being comprised of a set of component elements similar to the approach used earlier in this chapter in regard to the way the Du Pont model includes component elements.

c. Components of throughput include ① manufacturing cycle efficiency, ② process productivity, and ③ process quality yield.

$$\text{Manufacturing Cycle Efficiency} \times \text{Process Productivity} \times \text{Process Quality Yield} = \text{Throughput}$$

$$\frac{\text{Value-added Processing Time}}{\text{Total Time}} \times \frac{\text{Total Units}}{\text{Value-added Processing Time}} \times \frac{\text{Good Units}}{\text{Total Units}} = \frac{\text{Good Units}}{\text{Total Time}}$$

d. **Process productivity** is equal to the total units produced during a period using value-added processing time.

e. **Process quality yield** is the proportion of good units that resulted from the activities expended.

f. Companies are very concerned about the **cost of quality (COQ)**, and should therefore develop measurements related to COQ. (see text **Exhibit 16-10**)

D. **Activity-Based Costing and Performance Measurement**

1. Traditional performance measurements in accounting are replete with factors that contribute to non-value-added activities.

a. Materials standards are developed that include factors for waste.

b. Labor standards are developed that include an estimate of idle time.

c. Predetermined overhead rates are set using an estimate of expected capacity usage rather than full capacity usage.

d. Inventories are produced to meet budget expectations rather than sales demand.

2. Non-value-added (NVA) activities must be removed from performance evaluation measurements and value-added (VA) activities must be substituted if companies are to move toward world-class operations.

3. Performance measurements must be externally focused, must be linked to and support the business goals, and must measure what is of value to the customer.

E. Performance Evaluation in Multinational Settings

1. Upper level managers, in attempting to measure and evaluate overseas operations, usually focus on income as the overriding criterion in the evaluation all subunits, regardless of their locales. Such a singular focus is inappropriate for domestic responsibility centers and is even less appropriate for multinational segments.

2. Differences among cultures and economies are as important as differences in accounting standards and reporting practices when attempting to make comparisons of multinational organizational units.

3. The dollar amount of investments in different countries necessary to create the same type of organizational unit may differ substantially.

4. Income comparisons between multinational units may be invalid due to material differences in: (1) trade tariffs, (2) income tax rates, (3) currency fluctuations, and (4) the possibility of restrictions on the transfer of goods or currency from a country.

5. Income earned by a multinational unit may be affected by conditions totally outside the unit's control, such as (1) protectionism of local companies; (2) government aid in some countries; and (3) varying wage rates due to differing living standards, level of industrial development, and/or quantity of socialized services.

6. The diverse economic, legal/political, and tax structures of countries have affected the development and practice of accounting; the **International Accounting Standards Committee (IASC)** is working to achieve uniformity of accounting standards.

7. Managers may be able to transfer goods between segments at prices that minimize profits or tariffs in locations where taxes are high by shifting profits or cost values to more advantageous climates from a tax or tariff perspective.

8. U.S. firms having multinational profit or investment centers (or subsidiaries) need to establish flexible systems of measuring profit performance for those units.

   a. Such systems should recognize that differences in sales volumes, accounting standards, economic conditions, and risk may be outside the control of an international subunit's manager.

      b. Qualitative factors may become significantly more useful in such cases.

      c. Performance evaluations can include measures such as market share increases, quality improvements (defect reductions), establishment of just-in-time inventory systems with the related reduction in working capital, and new product development.

F. Relating Compensation and Performance

1. Many different employee compensation plans exist, and a rational compensation plan will tie its component elements together into a cohesive package. (see text **Exhibit 16-13**)

      a. The organizational strategic goals are determined by the board of directors and top management.

      b. The organization's critical success factors are identified from the strategic goals, and operational targets are then defined.

2. A **compensation strategy** is a foundation for the compensation plan that addresses the role compensation should play in the organization.

3. Automatic cost-of-living adjustments and annual pay raises are being reduced or eliminated; compensation plans need to encourage greater levels of employee performance and loyalty while lowering overall costs and raising profits.

4. The defined performance measures must be highly correlated with the organization's operational targets in structuring a **pay-for-performance plan**, or suboptimization may occur and workers could earn incentive pay even though the broader organizational objectives are not achieved..

      a. The first step in motivating employees to focus on productivity improvement involves correlating an organization's pay-for-performance plan with goals established in the strategic planning phase.

      b. The entire package of decisions regarding performance measurements can be referred to as a **performance management system**. (see text **Exhibit 16-14**)

      c. Pay-for-performance criteria should encourage employees to adopt a long-run perspective.

5. One school of thought advocates basing compensation on subjectively assessed intangible measures rather than the more objective performance-related measures.

6. The conventional compensation system has been primarily based on current monetary incentives.

   a. Middle managers are given salaries with the opportunity for future raises based on some, usually accounting-related, measure of performance such as segment margin or divisional ROI.

   b. Workers are paid wages for the number of hours worked or production level achieved; current or year-end bonuses may arise when performance is above some specified quantitative measure.

   c. Such a compensation system provides little motivation for employees who are not top managers to improve organizational performance.

7. An employee's organizational level and current compensation should affect the types of rewards chosen.

   a. Individuals at different employment levels usually perceive monetary rewards differently due to the relationship of pay to standard of living, and relative pay scales are vital to recognizing the value of monetary rewards to different employees.

   b. Incentives should be mostly monetary and short-term at lower employee levels, and incentives should be mostly nonmonetary and long-term at higher levels.

   c. Such a two-faceted compensation system provides lower-paid people with tangible rewards (more money) that directly enrich their lifestyles, but still provides rewards (such as stock options) that cause them to take a long-run "ownership" view of the organization.

   d. Highly paid top managers would receive more rewards (such as stock and stock options) that should impel them to be more concerned about the organization's long-term well-being rather than short-term personal gains.

8. The balancing of incentives provided for both groups (or teams) and individuals is also an important consideration in designing employee incentives.

   a. Workers in automated production systems function more by indirectly monitoring and controlling machinery and are therefore less directly involved in hands-on production.

   b. Incentives for small groups and individuals are often virtual substitutes; as the group grows larger, incentives must be in place for both the group and the individual.

   c. Group incentives are necessary to encourage cooperation among workers; and if *only* group incentives are offered, the incentive compensation system may be ineffective since the reward for individual effort goes to the group. The larger the size of the group, the smaller is the individual's share of the group reward.

   d. **Shirking** occurs when an individual free-rides on the group effort because the individual's share of the group reward is insufficient to compensate for his or her separate effort.

9. Employees may also be motivated by nonfinancial factors since there are human needs that cannot necessarily be satisfied by monetary wealth.

   a. Employees and managers will usually be more productive when they believe their efforts are appreciated, and modest gestures such as compliments and small awards can be used by superiors to recognize contributions of subordinates.

   b. Participation by subordinates in decisions affecting both their own welfare and the firm's welfare also contributes to making employment socially fulfilling.

   c. The concept of job security, which is so prevalent in Japanese firms, can be a compelling incentive.

10. Perceptions of disparity between the pay of ordinary workers and top managers has become a major issue of discussion and contention.

   a. Salary differentials between workers and CEOs are often created by a type of self-fulfilling prophecy caused by the board of directors, since the compositions of such boards is usually split between outsiders and insiders. Insiders are naturally more biased in favor of top management compensation than are outsiders.

   b. A company's board of directors will typically survey a group of similar organizations to determine the "average" compensation for an executive; if the company's executive appears to be underpaid, the board will increase his or her compensation.

G. **Global Compensation**

   1. An **expatriate** is a parent company or third-country national assigned to a foreign subsidiary or a foreign national assigned to the parent company.

   2. Compensation systems must be developed that compensate expatriate employees and managers on a fair and equitable basis as more companies engage in multinational operations.

      a. The compensation package paid to expatriates must reflect labor market factors, cost-of-living considerations, and currency fluctuations, as well giving consideration to tax consequences.

      b. Expatriates have an assortment of financial requirements and may therefore be paid in the currency of the country in which they reside, in the currency of their home country, or a combination of both.

      c. Price-level adjustment clauses are usually built into the compensation system in order to counteract any local currency inflation or deflation.

      d. The fringe benefit related to retirement must be aligned with the home country and should be paid in that currency, regardless of the currency makeup of the pay package.

      e. Income taxes are significant in the compensation package of expatriates since such individuals might pay taxes in the local country, home country, or both; some countries (like the United States and Great Britain) exempt expatriates from taxation on a specified amount of income earned in a foreign country.

Multiple Choice Questions from CMA Examinations

1. The imputed interest rate used in the residual income approach for performance measurement and evaluation can best be characterized as the:
   a. historical weighted average cost of capital for the company.
   b. marginal after-tax cost of new equity capital.
   c. average return on investment that has been earned by the company over a particular period.
   d. target return on investment set by management.
   e. average prime lending rate for the year being evaluated.

The correct answer is d. (CMA June 1981, 4-2)

TEACHING TRANSPARENCIES FOR RAIBORN MANAGERIAL ACCOUNTING 2ND EDITION

Number	TEACHING TRANSPARENCIES
1-1	American Exporters: Just Testing the Market?
1-2A	NAFTA: Better for U.S. Industry...
1-2B	...than for My Company?
2-1	Building a Better Baldrige
2-2	ISO 9000's Impact
2-3	Why Manufacturers are Becoming Certified
3-1	Most Manufacturers Believe American Industry Needs More Automation
3-2	Technology Use Growing Productivity and Automation
3-3	Quality Costs
3-4	Product Costs Flow T-Accounts
3-5	Summary of Accumulation of Production Costs
4-1	Relationships Among Capacity Measures
4-2	Product Cost Distortion
5-1	Assumptions of Activity-Based Costing
5-2	Activity Pools and Potential Cost Drivers
5-3	Definition of Cost Drivers
6-1A	Using Standard Costs
6-1B	
6-2A	Traditional Standard Cost System
6-2B	
6-2C	Updated Standard Cost System
6-2D	
6-2E	
6-3	Standard vs. Kaizen Costing
6-4A	Methods of Overhead Variance Analysis
6-4B	
6-4C	
7-1	Job Order and Process Costing Systems
7-2	Process and Job Order Costing Comparison
8-1	Variable and Absorption Costing Income Relationship
8-2	CVP Tendencies of Companies in the Same Industry Manufacturing the Same Product
8-3A	CVP and Inflation
8-3B	
8-4	CVP Graph
9-1	Illustration of Joint Process Output
9-2	Steps in Relevant Costing Decision Making
10-1	Budgeting – Planning and Controlling
11-1	The Budgeting Process
11-2	Master Budget Overview
11-3	Sales Budget
11-4	Production Budget (Manufacturing)
11-5	Purchases Budget (Sales)
11-6	Cash Budget
12-1	Evaluation Process
12-2	Budgeting and Control Cost Classifications
13-1	Types of Technologies in Use
13-2	The State of Automation
13-3	Manufacturers Welcome these Imports
14-1	Evaluating Capital Investments
15-1	Performance Management System
15-2	Transfer Pricing Methods Used by Respondent Firms
16-1A	Quality, Speed, or Price?
16-1B	
16-1C	
16-2	Appropriate Performance Measures
16-3	Financial Statement Ratios as Additional Performance Measures
16-4	Performance Measures and ABC

TEACHING TRANSPARENCY 1-1

AMERICAN EXPORTERS: JUST TESTING THE MARKET?

Does your firm export?

If Yes, what percent of sales are exports?

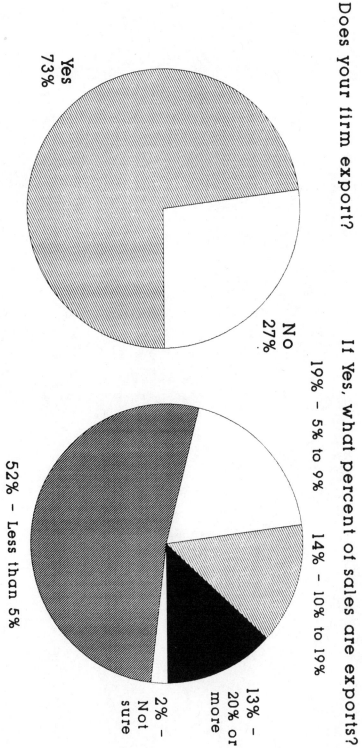

Yes 73%

No 27%

52% – Less than 5%

19% – 5% to 9%

14% – 10% to 19%

13% – 20% or more

2% – Not sure

Pie chart based upon 250 responses.

TEACHING TRANSPARENCY 1-2A
NAFTA: BETTER FOR U.S. INDUSTRY...

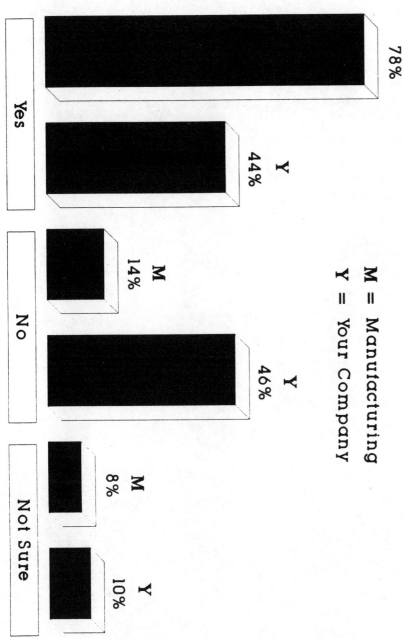

Would the North American Free Trade
Agreement benefit U.S. manufacturing in
general? Would it benefit your company?

M = Manufacturing
Y = Your Company

M
78%

Y
44%

M
14%

Y
46%

M
8%

Y
10%

Yes

No

Not Sure

TEACHING TRANSPARENCY 1-2B
...THAN FOR MY COMPANY?

Will NAFTA have a positive effect, negative effect, or no effect on your company?

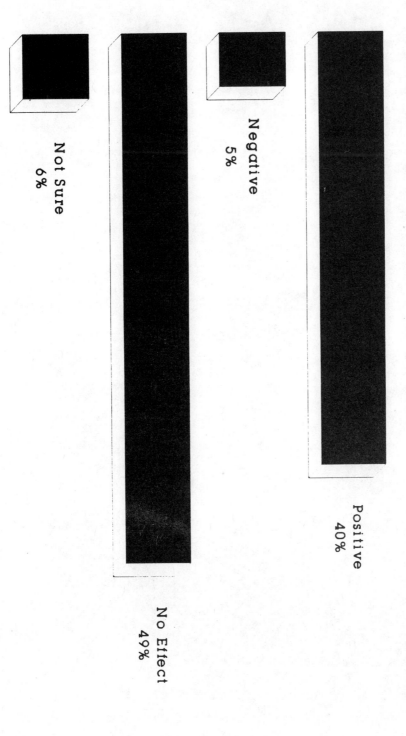

Positive
40%

No Effect
49%

Negative
5%

Not Sure
6%

BUILDING A BETTER BALDRIGE

Which of the following statements best describes your opinion of the Malcolm Baldrige National Quality Award?

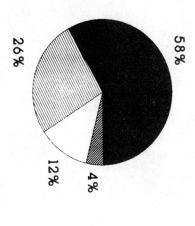

58%

26%

12%

4%

It is a good idea, but needs to address more substance than form regarding quality management.

It is a waste of time and money, by both the government and the companies that enter, and should be abandoned.

It helps U.S. manufacturers by promoting American product quality among prospective customers here and abroad.

No answer.

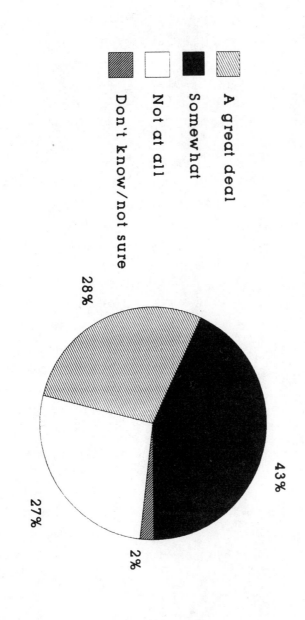

TEACHING TRANSPARENCY 2-2
ISO 9000'S IMPACT

Will these new standards affect your company?

A great deal

Somewhat

Not at all

Don't know/not sure

28%

43%

27%

2%

Based upon 172 responses.

TEACHING TRANSPARENCY 2-3
WHY MANUFACTURERS ARE BECOMING CERTIFIED

Which of the following contributed to your intention to certify under ISO 9000?

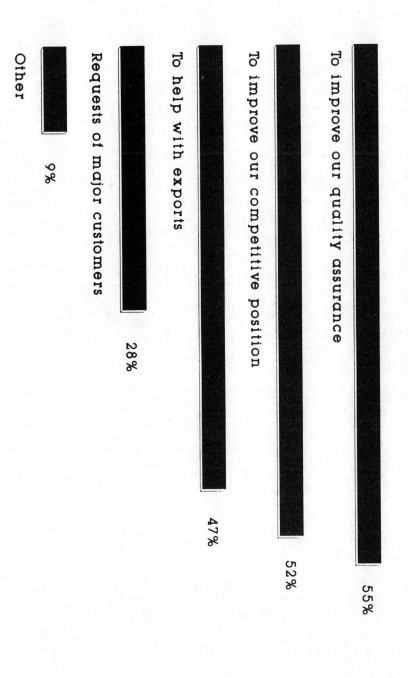

To improve our quality assurance   55%

To improve our competitive position   52%

To help with exports   47%

Requests of major customers   28%

Other   9%

Based upon 71 responses.
Multiple responses accepted.

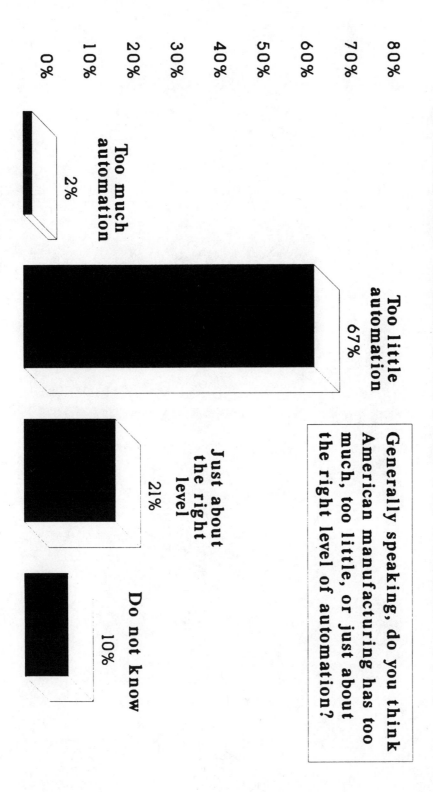

TEACHING TRANSPARENCY 3-1
MOST MANUFACTURERS BELIEVE AMERICAN
INDUSTRY NEEDS MORE AUTOMATION...

Generally speaking, do you think
American manufacturing has too
much, too little, or just about
the right level of automation?

Too little
automation
67%

Just about
the right
level
21%

Do not know
10%

Too much
automation
2%

80%
70%
60%
50%
40%
30%
20%
10%
0%

Note: Based opon 250 responses

TECHNOLOGY USE GROWING
PRODUCTIVITY AND AUTOMATION

The best way to improve
productivity is to automate

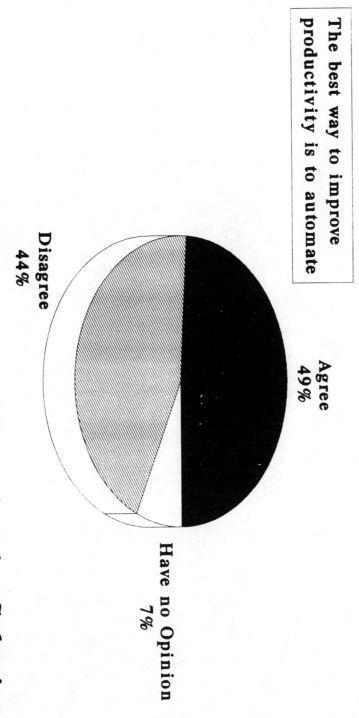

Disagree
44%

Agree
49%

Have no Opinion
7%

Automation Alone may not be the Solution

Note: Based upon 250 responses

QUALITY COSTS

Prevention
Costs

Appraisal
Costs

Failure
Costs

PRODUCT COSTS FLOW T-ACCOUNTS

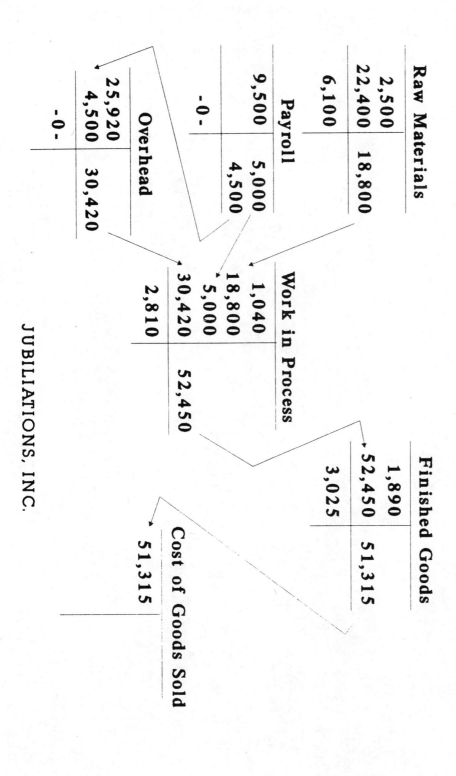

Raw Materials

2,500	
22,400	18,800
6,100	

Payroll

9,500	5,000
	4,500
-0-	

Overhead

25,920	30,420
4,500	
-0-	

Work in Process

1,040	
18,800	
5,000	
30,420	52,450
2,810	

Finished Goods

1,890	
52,450	51,315
3,025	

Cost of Goods Sold

51,315	

JUBILIATIONS, INC.

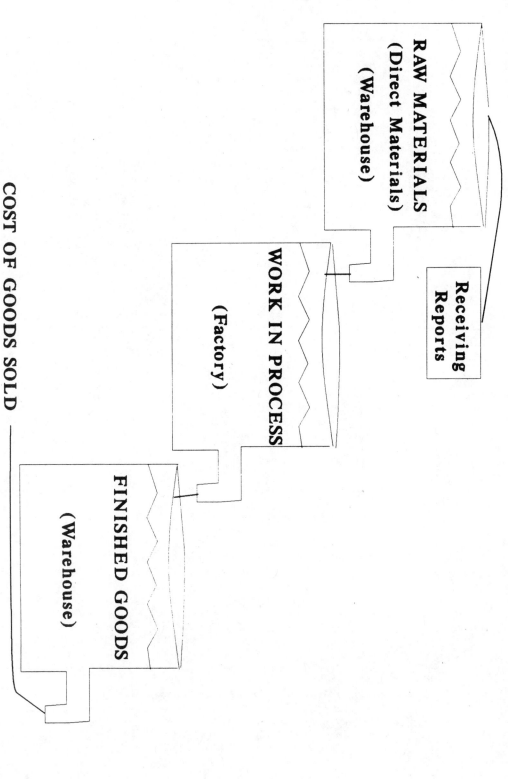

RAW MATERIALS
(Direct Materials)
(Warehouse)

Receiving
Reports

WORK IN PROCESS
(Factory)

FINISHED GOODS
(Warehouse)

COST OF GOODS SOLD

TEACHING TRANSPARENCY 4-1
RELATIONSHIPS AMONG CAPACITY MEASURES

Theoretical Capacity

Machine hours	600,000
Machine hours per unit.	3
Units	200,000

Unit

Variable product cost. . .	$ 30.00	$ 6,000,000
Fixed overhead applied. .	30.15	6,030,000
Total product cost.	$ 60.15	$ 12,030,000

Practical Capacity

Machine hours	510,000
Machine hours per unit.	3
Units	170,000

Unit

Variable product cost. . .	$ 30.00	$ 5,100,000
Fixed overhead applied. .	35.47	6,030,000
Total product cost.	$ 65.47	$ 11,130,000

Normal Capacity

Machine hours	450,000
Machine hours per unit.	3
Units	150,000

Unit

Variable product cost. . .	$ 30.00	$ 4,500,000
Fixed overhead applied. .	40.20	6,030,000
Total product cost.	$ 70.20	$ 10,530,000

Expected Capacity

Machine hours	480,000
Machine hours per unit.	3
Units	160,000

Unit

Variable product cost. . .	$ 30.00	$ 4,800,000
Fixed overhead applied. .	37.69	6,030,000
Total product cost.	$ 67.69	$ 10,830,000

PRODUCT COST DISTORTION

If total cost of goods sold are . . . .

Material	$	600
Labor		250
Overhead		1,000
Total	$1,850	

Most conventional cost accounting systems allocate Overhead on the basis of Labor

$$\frac{Overhead}{Labor} = \frac{\$1,000}{\$\ 250} = 400\%\ Overhead\ Rate$$

Resulting in a Reported Cost different from the True Cost consumed in making Product A and Product B . . . .

Product	True Cost		Recorded Cost	
	A	B	A	B
Material	$ 300	$ 300	$ 300	$ 300
Labor	50	200	50	200
Overhead	575	425	200	800
Total	$ 925	$ 925	$ 550	$1,300

A 41% error on both
Product A and B!

TEACHING TRANSPARENCY 5-1
ASSUMPTIONS OF ACTIVITY-BASED COSTING

- Activities consume resources.

- Products or customers consume activities.

- Model is consumption rather than spending.

- Resources consumed have numerous causes.

- Activities of wide array can be identified and measured.

- Cost pools are homogeneous.

- Costs in each pool are variable (strictly proportional to activity).

Activity Pools	Potential Cost Drivers
Engineering	Number of Drawing Changes
Purchasing	Number of Components; Number of Purchase Orders
Production Control	Number of Shop Orders; Number of Schedule Changes
Receiving	Number of Receipts
Quality	Number of Inspections; Amount of Scrap

DEFINITION OF COST DRIVERS

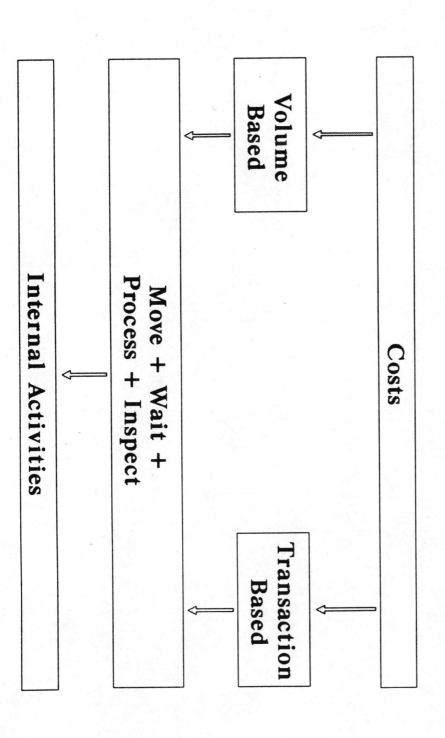

Costs

Volume
Based

Transaction
Based

Move + Wait +
Process + Inspect

Internal Activities

USING STANDARD COSTS

Standard cost systems are useful in companies that

- Produce a product or provide a service that can be assigned "norms" for quantities and/or costs
- Utilize a batch process
- Produce goods for which it is too expensive to determine actual product cost

Why are standard cost systems used?

- To gather the production costs for the company (cost accumulation)
- To determine and evaluate the performance of the company and its personnel (cost control)

This process requires an understanding of

- The process of setting the standards (Who was involved? How were measurements made? For what time period are they valid?)

- The degree of rigor underlying the standard (expected, practical, ideal)

- The party responsible for the variance (purchasing, production supervisor, personnel, engineering, external)

- The point in time at which the variance can be and is recognized and investigated

- The concept of management by exception

TRADITIONAL STANDARD COST SYSTEM

Inputs (pounds):

Actual pounds purchased..............................	2,700
Actual pounds used.......................................	2,600
Standard pounds per finished unit.............	2
Standard price per pound.............................	$ 1.00
Actual price per pound..................................	$ 1.10

Outputs (finished units):

Good units produced....................................	1,200

Standard cost per unit:

2 pounds @ $1 = $2

Standard cost variances:

Actual pounds purchased at actual
price (2,700 @ $1.10).. $ 2,970
Actual pounds purchased at standard
price (2,700 @ $1.00).. <2,700>
Purchase price variance - unfavorable
(2,700 @ $.10).. $ 270

Actual pounds used at standard price
(2,600 @ $1.00)... $2,600
Standard pounds allowed for good
production at standard price
([1,200 X 2] @ $1.00)... <2,400>
Quantity variance - unfavorable
(200 @ $1.00)... $ 200

UPDATED STANDARD COST SYSTEM

Inputs (pounds):

Actual pounds purchased..............................	2,700
Actual pounds used.......................................	2,600
Standard pounds per finished unit..............	2
Standard price per pound............................. $	1.00
Actual price per pound................................. $	1.10

Outputs (finished units):

Scheduled production..................................	1,000
Total production..	1,250
Good units produced....................................	1,200
Defective units..	50

Standard cost per unit:

2 pounds @ $1 = $2

Standard cost variances:
Input analysis:

Actual pounds used at actual price
(2,600 @ $1.10) .... $ 2,860

Actual pounds used at standard
price (2,600 @ $1.00) .... ⟨2,600⟩
_____

Price usage variance - unfavorable
(2,600 @ $.10) .... $ 260

Actual pounds used at standard
price (2,600 @ $1.00) .... $ 2,600

Standard pounds allowed for total
production at standard price
(1,250 X 2) @ $1.00) .... ⟨2,500⟩
_____

Quantity variance - unfavorable
(100 @ $1.00) .... $ 100

Output analysis:

Total production at standard cost
per unit (1,250 @ $2.00)............................. $ 2,500

Good units at standard cost per
unit (1,200 @ $2.00) .... <2,400>

Quality variance - unfavorable
(50 @ $2.00) .... $ 100

Good units at standard cost per
unit (1,200 @ $2.00) .... $ 2,400

Scheduled production at standard
cost per unit (1,000 @ $2.00) .... <2,000>

Production variance - unfavorable
(200 @ $2.00) .... $ 400

STANDARD VS. KAIZEN COSTING

Standard Costing Concepts	Kaizen Costing Concepts
Cost control system concept	Cost reduction system concept
Assume current manufacturing conditions	Assume continuous improvement in manufacturing
Meet cost performance standards	Achieve cost reduction targets
Standard Costing Techques	**Kaizen Costing Techniques**
Standards are set annually or semiannually	Cost reduction targets are set and applied monthly
	Continuous improvement (Kaizen) is implemented during the year to attain profit or to reduce the gap between target profit and estimated profit
Cost variance analysis involving standard costs and actual costs	Cost variance analysis involving target Kaizen costs and actual cost reduction amounts
Investigate and respond when standards are not met	Investigate and respond when target Kaizen amounts are not attained

TEACHING TRANSPARENCY 6-4A
METHODS OF OVERHEAD VARIANCE ANALYSIS

1 – way Analysis

	Actual	Applied
V	$ 7,402	$ 7,592
F	185,000	165,126
T	$192,402	$172,718

$ 19,684 U
Overhead Variance

2 – way Analysis

	Actual	Flexible 1	Applied
V	$ 7,402	$ 7,592	$ 7,592
F	185,000	190,530	165,126
T	$192,402	$198,122	$172,718

$ 5,720 F $ 25,404 U
Budget   Volume
Variance   Variance

$ 19,684 U
Overhead Variance

OLD ROSEBUD

METHODS OF OVERHEAD VARIANCE ANALYSIS

OLD ROSEBUD

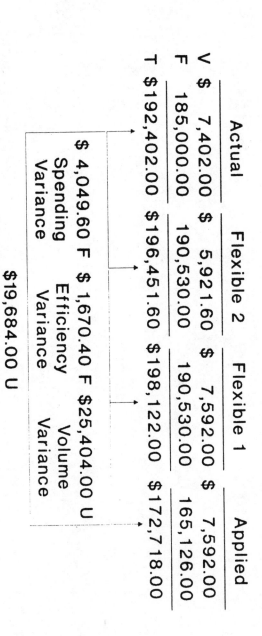

	3 - way Analysis

	Actual	Flexible 2	Flexible 1	Applied
V	$ 7,402.00	$ 5,921.60	$ 7,592.00	$ 7,592.00
F	185,000.00	190,530.00	190,530.00	165,126.00
T	$192,402.00	$196,451.60	$198,122.00	$172,718.00

$ 4,049.60 F	$ 1,670.40 F	$25,404.00 U
Spending	Efficiency	Volume
Variance	Variance	Variance

$19,684.00 U
Overhead Variance

METHODS OF OVERHEAD VARIANCE ANALYSIS

4 - way Analysis

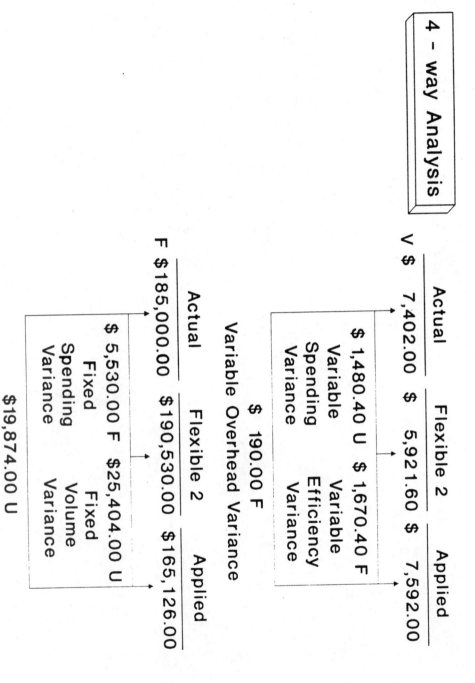

	Actual		Flexible 2		Applied
V $	7,402.00	$	5,921.60	$	7,592.00

$ 1,480.40 U $ 1,670.40 F

Variable Spending Variance

Variable Efficiency Variance

$ 190.00 F

Variable Overhead Variance

	Actual		Flexible 2		Applied
F $185,000.00		$190,530.00		$165,126.00

$ 5,530.00 F $25,404.00 U

Fixed Spending Variance

Fixed Volume Variance

$19,874.00 U

Fixed Overhead Variance

OLD ROSEBUD

Costing Systems

Job Order

- Small Quantities
- Specialized Jobs
- Products or Services
- Examples: Printing Shops
  and Tax
  Accountants

Process

- Large Quantities
- Homogeneous Products
- Products
- Example: Large
  Manufacturing
  Firms

PROCESS COSTING

WORK IN PROCESS

DIRECT MATERIALS
CONVERSION

→ PROCESS 1 ← PROCESS 2

PROCESS 2 → FINISHED GOODS → COST OF GOODS SOLD

JOB ORDER COSTING

WORK IN PROCESS

DIRECT MATERIALS
DIRECT LABOR
FACTORY OVERHEAD

→ JOB 1
→ JOB 2

JOB 1 → FINISHED GOODS → COST OF GOODS SOLD

JOB 2 →

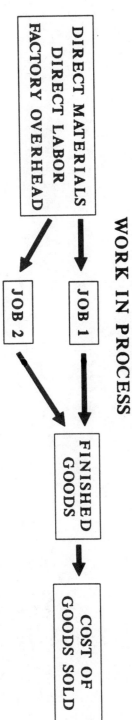

VARIABLE AND ABSORPTION COSTING
INCOME RELATIONSHIP

| Production = Sales | Variable Costing Income = Absorption Costing Income |

| Production > Sales | Variable Costing Income < Absorption Costing Income |

| Production < Sales | Variable Costing Income > Absorption Costing Income |

CVP TENDENCIES OF COMPANIES
IN THE SAME INDUSTRY
MANUFACTURING THE SAME PRODUCT

CVP Analysis Tool	Greater	Lesser
Degree of Operating Leverage	C-I	L-I
Breakeven Point	C-I	L-I
Margin of Safety	L-I	C-I
Contribution Margin Ratio	C-I	L-I
Cash Breakeven Point	C-I	L-I

C-I (Capital-Intensive) and L-I (Labor-Intensive)

CVP AND INFLATION

CVP analysis is just as effective when the effects of inflation are considered, as depicted in the following example.

No Inflation

	Unit	Breakeven
Units produced and sold.....		100,000
Sales.............................	$10.00	$1,000,000
Variable costs..................	<6.00>	<600,000>
Contribution margin..........	$ 4.00	$ 400,000
Fixed costs.....................		<400,000>
Operating income <loss>.....		$ -0-

	Unit	10% Inflation 100,000	Breakeven
Units produced and sold.....			
Sales..............	$11.00	$1,100,000	
Variable costs........	<6.60>	<660,000>	
Contribution margin........	$ 4.40	$ 440,000	
Fixed costs............		<440,000>	
Operating income <loss>.....		$ -0-	

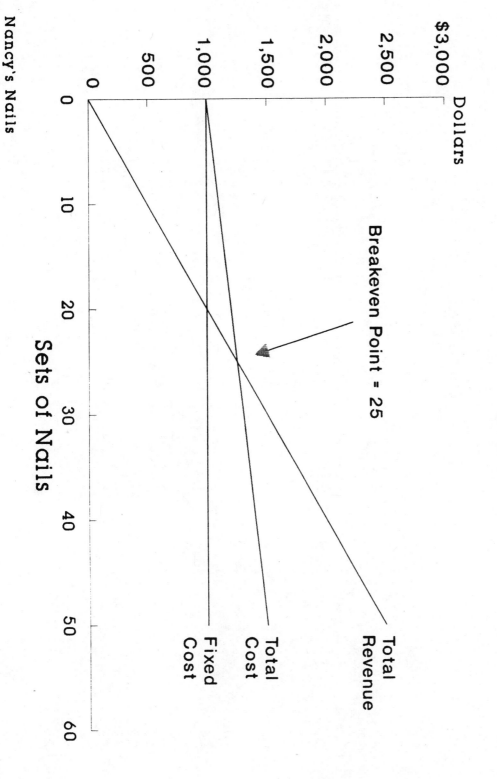

TEACHING TRANSPARENCY 8-4
CVP GRAPH

Dollars

$3,000

2,500

2,000

1,500

1,000

500

0

Breakeven Point = 25

Total
Revenue

Total
Cost

Fixed
Cost

0   10   20   30   40   50   60

Sets of Nails

Nancy's Nails

ILLUSTRATION OF JOINT PROCESS OUTPUT

Raw Material
Input -
Fresh Corn

Joint Process -
Shucking and
Cleaning

Joint Process
Outputs

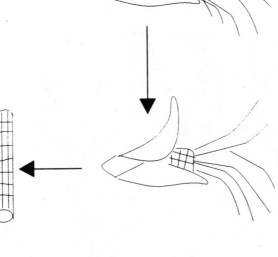
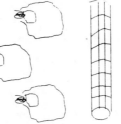

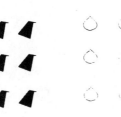

Corn-on-the Cob
(Joint Product) will
be bagged and sold

Whole Kernels
(Joint Product) will
be added to
sugar-water,
canned, and sold

Partial Kernels
(By-product) will be
ground to make
corn meal or grits
and sold

Inferior Kernels
(Scrap) will be sold
to animal food
producers

Cobs (Waste) will
be discarded

STEPS IN RELEVANT COSTING DECISION MAKING

Step	
1	Define the problem.
2	Recognize the alternatives
3	Determine the cost and benefits associated with each alternative.
4	Collect the data.
5	Total the relevant costs and benefits for each alternative.
6	Make the decision.

TEACHING TRANSPARENCY 10-1
BUDGETING - PLANNING AND CONTROLLING

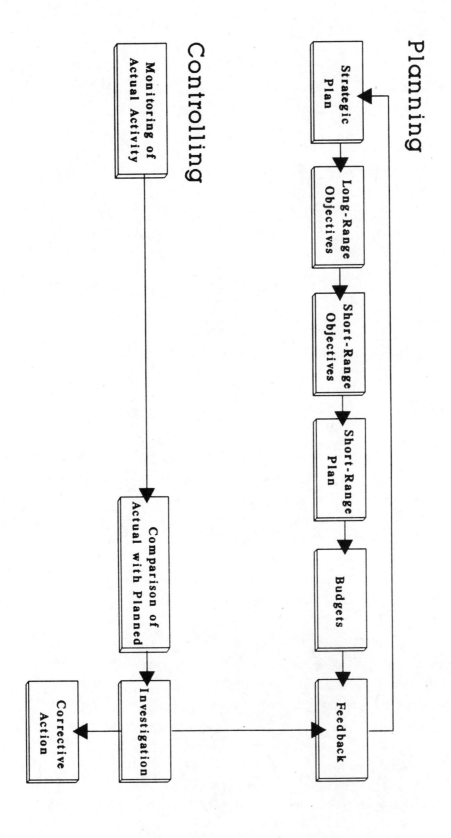

Planning

| Strategic Plan → Long-Range Objectives → Short-Range Objectives → Short-Range Plan → Budgets → Feedback |

Controlling

Monitoring of Actual Activity → Comparison of Actual with Planned → Investigation → Corrective Action

THE BUDGETING PROCESS

SET GOALS AND OBJECTIVES

- Achievement of desired goals and objectives requires complex activities, uses diverse resources, and necessitates formalized planning.

ANALYZE KEY VARIABLES

- Key variables can be internal or external.

GATHER RELEVANT DATA

- Information related to the key variables can be gathered.

DETERMINE UNDERLYING ASSUMPTIONS ABOUT PROJECTED CHANGES IN KEY VARIABLES

- Assumptions are then made about changes that may occur in the key variables during the planning period.

INPUT DATA INTO BUDGET MODEL

- Employee participation is essential if the budgeting process is to be effective.

THE BUDGET

- Budget implementation means that the budget is now considered a standard against which performance can be measured.

MASTER BUDGET OVERVIEW

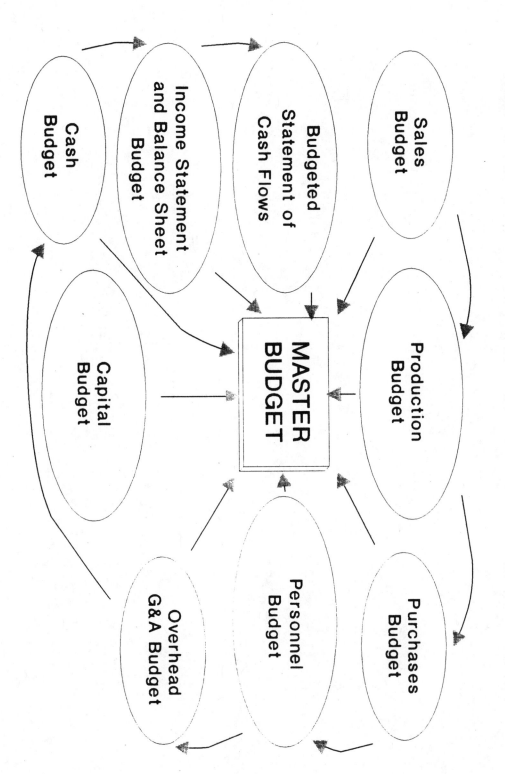

SALES BUDGET

Factors in Sales Forecasting

- Past Sales Volumes
- Seasonal Variations
- Economic/Industry Conditions
- Competition
- Market Research Studies
- Sales Force Quality

- Pricing Policies
- Production/Storage Capacity
- Long-Term Trends
- Relative Product Profitability
- Advertising and Promotion

PRODUCTION BUDGET (MANUFACTURING)

From Sales Budget	To Production Budget	
Sales in Units	Sales in Units	XXX
Item 1 XX	+ Desired Ending Inventory	XXX
Item 2 XX	= Total Units Needed	XXX
Sales in Dollars	- Beginning Inventory	<XXX>
Item 1 $ XX	= Units to be Produced	XXX
Item 2 XX		
Total Sales $ XX		

Total units needed will be the sum of the desired ending inventory plus the amount needed to fulfill budgeted sales - part of which will be met by beginning inventory.

Budget applies to the manufacturing profit center only.

PURCHASES BUDGET (SALES)

From Sales Budget		To Purchases Budget	
Sales in Units		Units to be Sold	XXX
Item 1	xx	+ Desired Ending Inventory	XXX
Item 2	xx	= Total Whole Quantities Needed	XXX
Sales in Dollars		– Beginning Inventory	<XXX>
Item 1	$ xx	= Purchases Required	XXX
Item 2	xx		
Total Sales	$ xx		

Since the store will be purchasing finished goods, a production budget is not prepared.

CASH BUDGET

	JAN	FEB	MAR
Beginning cash balance	$ XXX	$ XXX	$ XXX
Cash collections	XXX	XXX	XXX
Cash available (exclusive of financing)	$ XXX	$ XXX	$ XXX
Disbursements:			
Accounts payable	$ XXX	$ XXX	$ XXX
Direct labor	XXX	XXX	XXX
Overhead	XXX	XXX	XXX
General and administrative expenses	XXX	XXX	XXX
Total planned disbursements	$ XXX	$ XXX	$ XXX
Cash excess ‹deficit›	$ XXX	$ XXX	$ XXX
Minimum cash balance desired	XXX	XXX	XXX
Cash available or needed	$ XXX	$ XXX	$ XXX
Financing:			
Borrowings ‹repayments›	$ XXX	$ XXX	$ XXX
Liquidate ‹acquire› plant assets	XXX	XXX	XXX
Receive ‹pay› interest	XXX	XXX	XXX
Total impact of planned financing	XXX	XXX	XXX
Ending cash balance	$ XXX	$ XXX	$ XXX

EVALUATION PROCESS

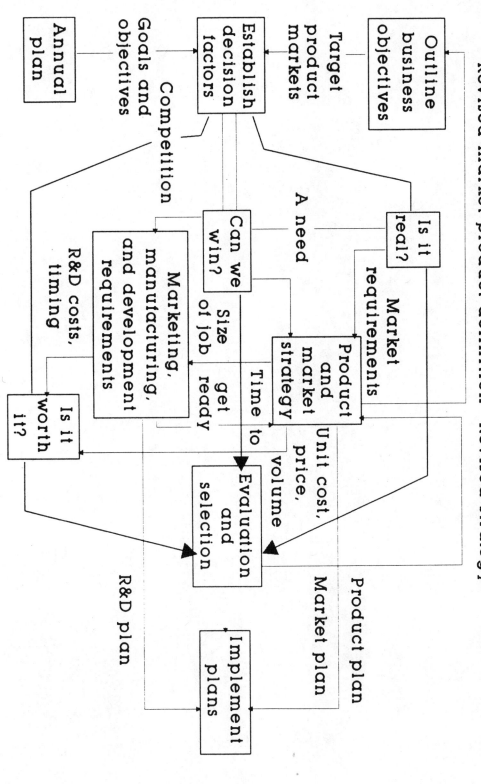

BUDGETING AND CONTROL COST CLASSIFICATIONS

Cost Classification	Period of Time for Budgeting and Feedback	Primary Accounting Control Methods
Engineered	Short	Standards and Flexible Budgets
Discretionary	Long	Negotiated Fixed Budgets
Committed	Longer	Capital Expenditure Budgets

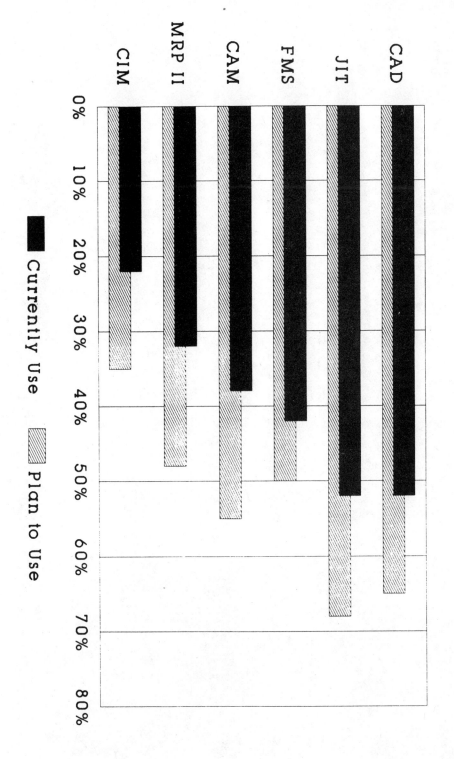

TEACHING TRANSPARENCY 13-1

TYPES OF TECHNOLOGIES IN USE

■ Currently Use   ▨ Plan to Use

CAD
JIT
FMS
CAM
MRP II
CIM

0% 10% 20% 30% 40% 50% 60% 70% 80%

THE STATE OF AUTOMATION

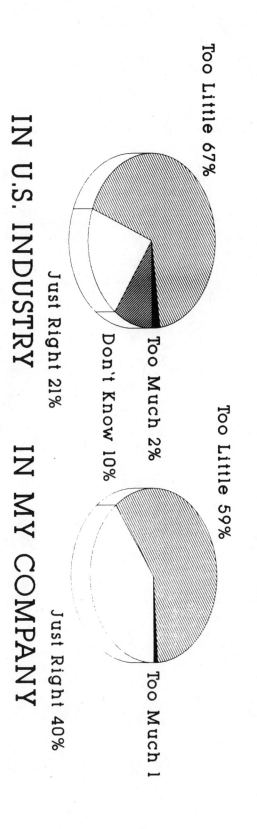

IN U.S. INDUSTRY

Too Little 67%

Just Right 21%

Don't Know 10%

Too Much 2%

IN MY COMPANY

Too Little 59%

Just Right 40%

Too Much 1

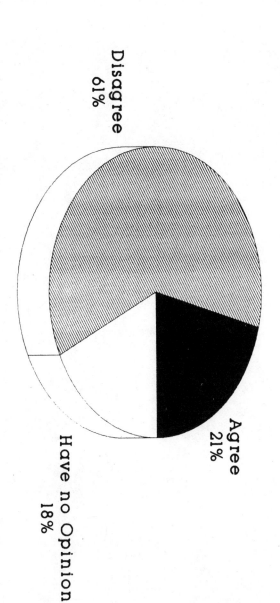

Disagree
61%

Agree
21%

Have no Opinion
18%

Japanese management techniques don't
work in the United States.

Note: Based upon 250 responses

TEACHING TRANSPARENCY 14-1
EVALUATING CAPITAL INVESTMENTS

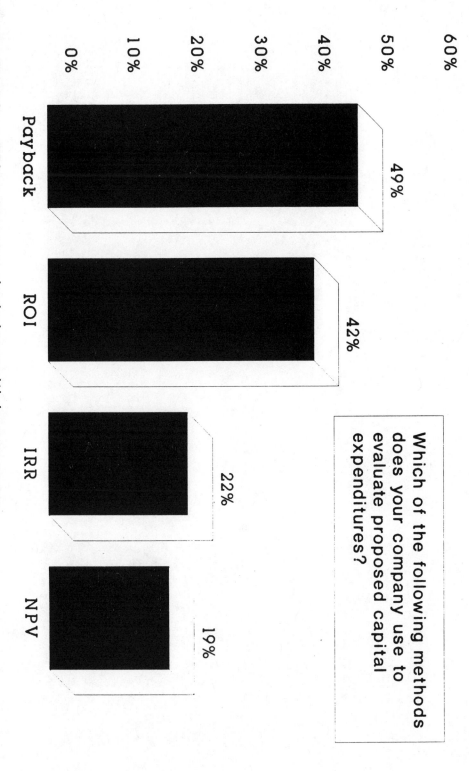

Which of the following methods does your company use to evaluate proposed capital expenditures?

Payback 49%

ROI 42%

IRR 22%

NPV 19%

Note: Based on 250 responses. Includes multiple responses.

PERFORMANCE MANAGEMENT SYSTEM

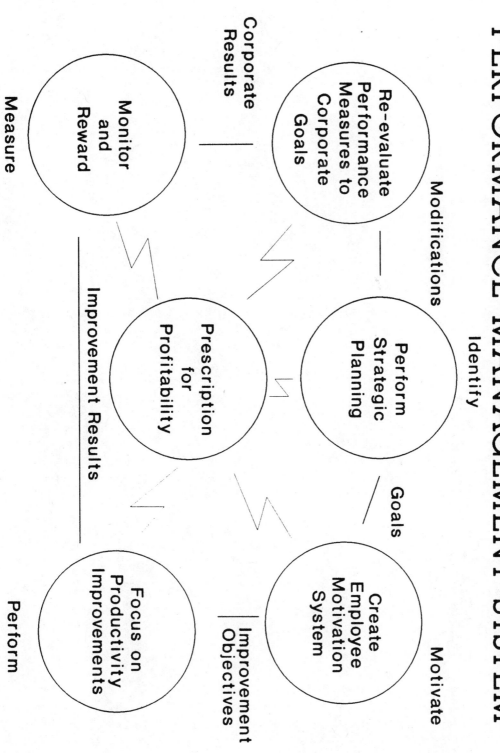

TEACHING TRANSPARENCY 15-2
TRANSFER PRICING METHODS USED BY RESPONDENT FIRMS

Pricing Methods	Domestic # of Firms	Domestic Percent	International # of Firms	International Percent
Cost-based transfer prices:				
Actual or standard variable cost of production	8	3.59	2	1.27
Actual full production cost	20	8.97	6	3.82
Standard full production cost	34	15.25	11	7.01
Actual variable production cost plus a lump-sum subsidy	2	.90	2	1.27
Full production cost (actual or standard) plus a markup	37	16.59	42	26.75
Other	2	.90	2	1.27
Market-based transfer prices:				
Market price	56	25.11	41	26.12
Market price less selling expenses	17	7.62	19	12.10
Other	9	4.04	12	7.65
Negotiated price	37	16.59	20	12.74
Other methods	1	.44	0	.00
Totals	223 *	100.00	157 *	100.00

*Many firms use more than one transfer price.

QUALITY, SPEED, OR PRICE?

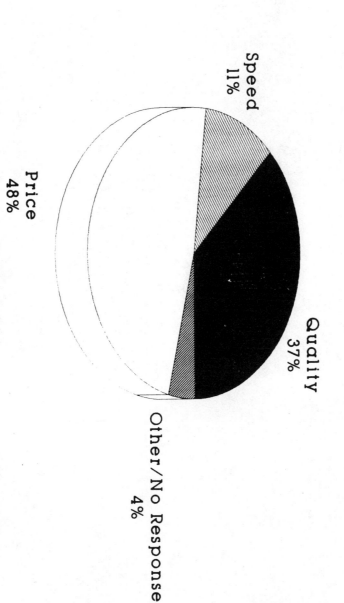

Speed
11%

Price
48%

Quality
37%

Other/No Response
4%

Many mid-sized manufacturers say they compete on price...

Note: Based upon 250 responses

QUALITY, SPEED, OR PRICE?

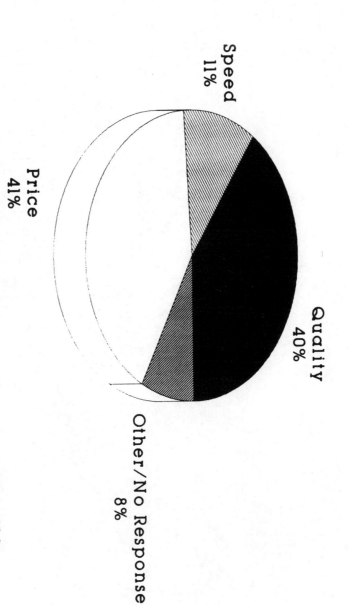

Speed
11%

Price
41%

Quality
40%

Other/No Response
8%

but those who are optimistic on profits
are more likely to compete on quality...

Note: Based upon responses from 114
manufacturers who expected 1990
profits to increase.

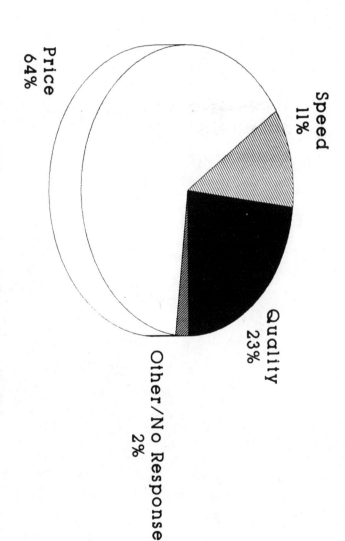

TEACHING TRANSPARENCY 16-1C
QUALITY, SPEED, OR PRICE?

Speed
11%

Price
64%

Quality
23%

Other/No Response
2%

than those who are pessimistic.

Note: Based upon responses from 44
manufacturers who expected 1990
profits to decrease.

APPROPRIATE PERFORMANCE MEASURES

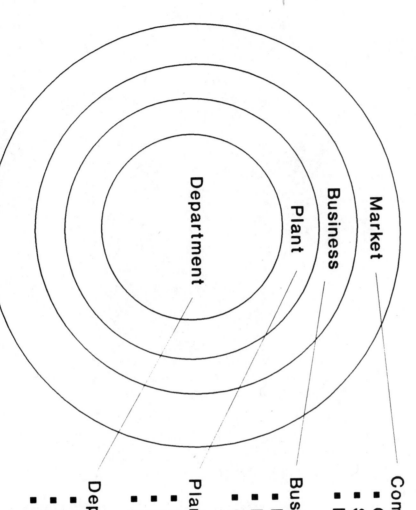

Market
Business
Plant
Department

Competitive Position
- Quality
- Service
- Life Cycle

Business Performance
- Net Income
- Return
- Cash Flow

Plant Performance
- Cost
- Quality
- Inventory

Department
- Setup
- Down Time
- Throughput Time

FINANCIAL STATEMENT RATIOS
AS ADDITIONAL PERFORMANCE MEASURES

Current Ratio:

$$\frac{\text{Current Assets}}{\text{Current Liabilities}}$$

Acid-Test Ratio:

$$\frac{\text{Quick Assets}}{\text{Current Liabilities}}$$

Accounts Receivable Turnover:

$$\frac{\text{Net Sales on Account}}{\text{Average Accounts Receivable}}$$

Average Collection Period:

$$\frac{\text{365 Days}}{\text{Accounts Receivable Turnover}}$$

Inventory Turnover:

$$\frac{\text{Cost of Goods Sold}}{\text{Average Inventory}}$$

Asset Turnover:

$$\frac{\text{Net Sales}}{\text{Average Total Assets}}$$

Times Interest Earned:

$$\frac{\text{Earnings before Interest Expense and Income Taxes}}{\text{Interest Expense}}$$

Debt-to-Equity Ratio:

$$\frac{\text{Total Liabilities}}{\text{Stockholders' Equity}}$$

PERFORMANCE MEASURES AND ABC

- Conventional systems measure financial performance and some non-financial measures at the product level.

- The conventional measures do not identify the factors that directly measure performance.

- Activity-based performance measures the factors that directly affect the output of each activity.

- All of the performance factors are interdependent. Changes in one factor will result in changes in one or more of the other factors.

- The goal is to achieve improvements in all factors simultaneously.

- The performance measures can then be analyzed to identify ways in which the performance can be improved.